Help!

**For Parents of Infants
from Birth to Six Months**

By Parents for Parents

**Vol. 1
The Suggestion Circle Series**

Edited by

**Jean Illsley Clarke,
Samara Kemp,
Gail Nordeman,
and Ellen Peterson**

1817

Harper & Row, Publishers, San Francisco

Cambridge, Hagerstown, New York, Philadelphia, Washington
London, Mexico City, São Paulo, Singapore, Sydney

To all the babies

The developmental affirmations for children on page 14 are adapted from Pamela Levin's therapeutic affirmations in *Becoming the Way We Are* and are used with the permission of the author.

Cover design: Terry Dugan
Illustrations: Jerry Smath

Library of Congress Cataloging-in-Publication Data

Help! for parents of infants from birth to six months.

(The Suggestion circle series; vol. 1)
Includes index.
1. Infants—Care and hygiene—United States.
2. Child rearing—United States.   I. Clarke, Jean Illsley.
II. Parents for parents.   III. Series.
HQ774.H45 1986   649'.122   86-18383
ISBN 0-86683-451-6

87 88 89 90 OPM 10 9 8 7 6 5 4 3 2

Contents

CLUSTERS AND SUGGESTION CIRCLES

Appreciations

For the wealth of circles you gave to us, we thank

- The Nurture Company and Parent Infant Education classes, the Acalanes Adult Center, and the "Self- Esteem: A Family Affair" classes in Lafayette and Walnut Creek, California.
- The "Mothers Retreat" participants at Westerbeke Ranch.
- The people from the Healdsburg group.
- The Modesto Junior College group of young parents and their babies.
- The "Self-Esteem: A Family Affair" support groups, and especially Steve and Mary Dunn, Shari Miller, Ed and Karyl Sakir, Yvette Podlogar, Diane Karsh, Eileen Burt, Meg Murray, Don DuPont, Rose Chait, Jason Davis, Annette Holmberg, Jane Kincaid, Nanette Mills, Kathy and Bart Simmons, Mike and Donna Spoon, Joan Hobbs, Karen Hobbs, Cal and Beth Darrow, Eileen and Mark Pleticha, Sandie Wood, Sally Shepherd, Suzanne Perot, Grace Sample, Linda Bell, Beverly Konkin, Alison Horlak, Dee Corbett, and Alison Pomatto.

For reading the manuscript and offering us their wisdom, we thank Annye Rothenberg and Alice Van Der Laan.

For connecting abuse with lack of knowledge about child development and for editing the book for medical accuracy, we thank pediatrician, Christine Ternand.

For their support, dedication, and humor we thank Becky Monson, Mary Ann Lisk, Nancy Nenovich, and Vivian Rouson-Gossett.

Especially from Gail: To Harold, my husband, who said, "Do it, Gail!" To the hundreds of couples who have shared the birth of their babies with me, to my colleagues in Childbirth Education and Transactional Analysis, to the continual rebirth of the infant within myself, and to my own children.

Especially from Samara: To my children, Shawni, Darren, Brett, and Brad for their patience, support, and devotion. Many thanks to my dear friend and confidant, Johanna Blest, who first introduced me to my coauthors. Also I am grateful to my wide circle of friends, who gave suggestions, listened when I needed them, and offered positive messages.

Especially from Ellen: To Jean Clarke for introducing the Suggestion Circle technique to so many, to moms in class I've come to love as sisters, and to my precious family--Al, Andy, and Katherine for sharing our home with the editorial team.

Especially from Jean: To Deane Gradous for suggesting we collect these valuable circles and publish them, to Ellen Peterson for being the first editor to volunteer, and to my family for their laughter and encouragement.

—The Editors

Foreword

This book, written by and for parents, seems to be the first of its kind. It employs a question-and-answer format, but it departs from the traditional mold in that the so-called experts are only foot-noted, should readers wish to explore some topics further. The *parents*, in fact, are the real experts as they come together in Suggestion Circles that have been organized and led by the book's editors and their colleagues. The questions in the book reflect the many concerns of new parents, and there are no "right" answers. Each parent must find his or her own way.

The editors' rich blend of personal and profes-sional experience includes transactional analysis theory, and the book draws on the self-esteem affirmations included in Jean Illsley Clarke's *Self- Esteem: A Family Affair*. These concepts come through in the organization and content of the book, and they add to the ease and pleasure of the reader.

The chapters in *HELP! for Parents of Infants from Birth to Six Months* are organized around the concerns of most new parents, so this should be a useful resource. Busy parents can easily find their topic of interest and mull over the many answers to each question before deciding what feels right for them. For this reason, the book is not guilt-producing; it supports all parents' right to choose and find their own way.

Since the first six months of a child's life are particularly stressful for new parents, it should be comforting for a parent to know that other parents worry about the same child-rearing issues. The many answers to each question give parents comfort, if not courage, in knowing that they are not alone in their worries. A commonsense approach to child-rearing is therefore encouraged. Parents can try on each answer to a question and, if it fits, use it. The experience may help them recognize that the answers to most questions are within themselves.

Finally, the book is especially appropriate and helpful for parents today because of its emphasis on coparenting, treating the father as equal, and respecting the rights of everyone in the family.

—Earladeen Badger, Ph.D.
Associate Professor of Pediatrics
Director, Infant/Toddler Learning Program
University of Cincinnati Children's Hospital
Medical Center

What Is This Book About?

This is a book written for parents by parents.

It is a book for the days when you don't know what to do or when what you're doing isn't working. It does *not* have a lot of theory, and it is not for times when things are going smoothly. It *is* a book of specific, practical suggestions for handling different problems that parents have sought help with in parenting classes around the country.

These parents attended either "Self-Esteem: A Family Affair" classes, led by specially trained facilitators, or other groups led by those same facilitators. Participants in all these meetings used a technique called the "Suggestion Circle" to collect options for parents with problems. Class members sit in a circle and listen to a parent describe a problem. Each member of the Circle then offers his or her best suggestion for solving it. In this way, the person with the problem benefits from the collective wisdom and experience of the whole group and goes home with a list of suggestions or options.

The Suggestion Circle process is different from brainstorming, which encourages people to offer every idea they can imagine. It's also different from listening to the teacher or the expert provide "the correct answer." In a Suggestion Circle, *every* answer comes from the experience of a parent, grandparent, day-care provider, or teacher. Each answer represents the best suggestion that person had to offer.

We chose these eighty-seven Circles because they present problems we hear repeatedly and that seem to be particularly difficult for parents. Leaders collected the suggestions and asked the parents if we could share their responses with you in these books. You'll see that some of the suggestions include references to positive messages, called "Affirmations," and to Pam Levin's theory of recycling. These concepts are part of the "Self-Esteem: A Family Affair" class. Parents have found affirmations helpful and the theory of recycling hopeful, so they suggested that we include a short description of those two concepts. We have done that.

We have dropped any ideas that advocated violence both because child abuse is illegal and because we do not believe violence helps children. We also eliminated suggestions that implied that a problem was not serious or worthy of a parent's best effort, because we assume that if parents ask for help, the problems are important to them.

You will find the Suggestion Circles grouped in clusters according to subject matter. Each Circle includes the name of the first facilitator who sent the problem to us and the location of that class. Since similar problems come up in different parts of the country, we have combined suggestions from more than one group. Note that these suggestions were gathered from parents of generally healthy babies without special physical or sensitivity problems.

So here they are, some short reference pieces and eighty-seven circles—eighty-seven collections of the best ideas from parents who have been there, to you who are there now.

—The Editors

How to Use This Book

You can use this book to help you solve problems. When you want ideas, look in the table of contents for a cluster title that seems to include your problem. For example, if you have a fussy baby, look under the cluster title "Crying." Or look in the index for words that describe your problem (like *fussing*, *crying*, *colic*) and read about the problems that sound most like yours.

Reading about what other parents have done will remind you that there are many ways to solve problems and that you can try out new things and find ways that work for you and your baby. If you read a list over several times, you will probably see ideas that you didn't notice before.

Some of the suggestions may not fit your situation or your parenting style. Some of the lists contain contradictions, since there are many healthy ways to raise children. Remember that these suggestions are *not* listed in any order of importance. Think about which suggestions sound useful to you.

Whenever you think of a suggestion that is not listed, write it in your book for future reference. Our purpose is not to give "one right answer" but to support and stimulate your search to find your own workable answer by offering the wisdom of hundreds of the real child-rearing experts—parents themselves.

This is a book to dip into again and again, not to read straight through. Read the sections at the beginning and the end, and then read the Circles as you need them.

- For a picture of normal infant behavior, read **Ages and Stages**. You can use it to check out whether your expectations are reasonable.
- To help your baby learn to trust, look at **Affirmations for Growth**. You can ponder these healthy messages and consider how to encourage your infant to decide to trust, to "be," to bond with you. Use your own words, expressions, touch, and attention to give these messages.
- Should you wonder whether you are neglecting your baby, read **Abuse and Neglect**.
- If you have noticed that you would like lots of care and support or that you are emotionally tender, read **Parents Get Another Chance— Recycling**.

Honor yourself for the many things you do well with your children. Celebrate your growth and theirs, and change when you need to.

Note: Throughout this book, we have alternated masculine and feminine pronouns; in one section or Circle, the child will be a "she," in the next a "he." In each case, please read "all children."

—Jean Illsley Clarke and Ellen Peterson

Ages and Stages

No baby in the world is just like yours. Nature's pattern for development is universal, but each baby has his own style and timing. Here are some examples:

- No two days are alike: sleeping and eating times may vary widely.
- Babies have likes and dislikes from day one.
- Some babies want to be held and carried almost all the time; others don't.
- Some babies like vigorous handling; some like to be handled gently.
- Some babies lie quietly and observe their world; others wave and kick like cyclists.
- Some babies poop every time they eat; some poop every couple of days.
- Boys and girls are different from the start in many more ways than just their genitalia.
- Some babies reject everyone's care but Mom's for now.
- Few babies can simply be put to bed. Most must suck, cry, or be rocked first.
- Their sucking urge is so strong that it is usually not satisfied during feedings alone.
- Most babies cry for two or more hours of the twenty-four.
- Babies are often fussiest during evening hours.
- Colic is intense crying for extended times throughout the day. Babies usually outgrow it by four months.

- Some babies are easy, and some are just plain hard to live with at first.
- Babies are learning all the time. They imitate and differentiate and categorize.
- Babies begin language with lots of different sounds. They imitate human sounds, rather than the clock or refrigerator. They concentrate on the sounds of their parents' speech: Swedish babies focus on Swedish sounds.
- They like to look at faces, especially eyes. They can see clearly about ten inches away at birth— just the distance for focusing on your face when cradled in your arms.
- They become extremely distressed when parents break a normal, happy exchange and stare blankly at them without speaking.
- Babies have a variety of smiles, including a special one for Mom and Dad. Others smile after solving a problem, for strangers, and in relief after realizing that something frightening is not really threatening.
- They learn very fast, perhaps taking in and assimilating more information in the first six months than in any other similar stretch of time.
- Babies need to keep you close, so they come packaged with several traits that make it rewarding for you to stay near them. Parents need not fear that open, unabashed displays of affection will "spoil" an infant.
- Their skin invites caressing, and their cheeks are made for kissing.
- They fit perfectly in your arms.

- They like an easy transition from the womb; they respond to hearing Mom's heartbeat, feeling warmth, enjoying being swaddled, being walked.
- They don't have adult motives like revenge or "teaching you a lesson."
- They are forgiving.
- They display relief when you are dependable.
- They are wonderfully cute and fascinating.

Reading your baby's clues and responding to them effectively will help you make a good beginning together. Keep your baby close, learn with him, protect him, and celebrate love.

—Ellen Peterson

About Abuse and Neglect

Child abuse and neglect are prevalent and perhaps epidemic in our society today. We feel strongly that all children are to be valued and cherished. We believe that children will be better protected when parents know the causes and signs of child abuse and when they learn ways to keep children safe.

Causes of Child Abuse

There are many causes of child abuse. Since this is not a book about the ills of society or emotionally disturbed individuals but about normal, healthy parents and children, we will address only the abuse that springs from parents' misunderstanding of the normal growth and development of children at different ages. As children go about their developmental tasks, they sometimes do things that are misinterpreted by parents, who may be overly severe or hurtful in their attempts to stop or control these behaviors. Parents may believe that they are "disciplining," but when they punish their children for doing what is developmentally correct and normal, children are hurt physically or emotionally.

The following behaviors or characteristics of children this age are frequently misunderstood:
• Extended periods of crying. An infant cries to let you know she has a need. A baby should be learning to trust those important to her. She

needs *unconditional love* and *caretaking*. Her needs may seem exhausting or even overwhelming to a caring adult. (The caring adults must realize that adults require adequate support in order to meet the infant's needs, because tired adults may act and speak abusively despite their best intentions.)

- Wakeful at night. Infants frequently take three to six weeks to establish a normal light/dark sleep cycle. (The womb was always dark.) They are not deliberately trying to keep the adult exhausted by being active at night. They may need guidance to help synchronize their sleeping and waking periods to match those of the rest of the family.

- Grabbing and biting. Babies have strong reflexes for sucking and grasping, and they may inadvertently cause parents physical pain by pulling hair, grabbing skin, or biting. Parents may misinterpret these reflexes as willful attempts to hurt, and they may respond harshly or hurt the child back. Parents need to remember that only nurturing touch should be used with the baby.

- Being real, not ideal. The difference between the ideal baby (or the "Gerber baby") and the baby the parents bring home is often difficult for parents to accept. They may mistakenly try to fit their baby into the "Gerber image" instead of accepting the child as she is. At this age the child should be learning and simply being herself. Well-meaning parents may inappropriately try to get their child to "do things" (e.g., raise

10

her head, smile, look at flash cards, etc.) before the time she would do them naturally. Parents should celebrate the new life and be with the child, not push the infant to perform.

- Being male or female. Since the child needs to experience unconditional acceptance, the sex of the child must be accepted and affirmed. If you wished for a child of the other sex, accept this child as fast as you can. Enjoy boys for being boys and girls for being girls, and encourage others to do the same.

Signs of Abuse

How can you tell if your child has been abused by others? The following are sometimes signs of abuse:

- A child who is not gaining weight or length.
- Diaper rash that's getting worse or is not clearing up when the child is in the care of others.
- Pin-size marks around the eyes or blood in the white part of the eye, which may indicate that the child has been shaken.
- Circular bite marks, either adult- or child-size.
- Hand-slap marks on the face or elsewhere.
- Bruises.

Ways to Protect Your Infant

We keep babies safe and physically protected when we

- refuse to leave a child alone in a house or car;
- always use car seats when traveling with a child in a car;

- use safe toys, cribs, and other infant equipment;
- carefully supervise a baby on a dressing table, in an infant seat or swing, and in a shopping cart;
- set firm limits on a babysitter's activities, and remind the sitter that the infant comes first; and
- allow other young children to be around the baby only with constant supervision.

We assure physical and emotional security when we meet our infants' needs with respect and caring. Infants learn to trust when we provide the following:

- Adequate food but not overfeeding. If you are bottle-feeding a child, the child should be held and given eye contact during feedings; he should not be left with a propped bottle.
- Touch, including frequent skin-to-skin, not just skin-to-clothing, contact. Touch that hurts, such as pinching a baby's cheeks, is not appropriate.
- Warm clothing. Dressing the child as warmly or as lightly as you dress yourself is a convenient rule of thumb.
- Prompt attention to distress. Children should never cry for more than fifteen minutes without an adult going to reassure them.
- Dry diapers. Some children are more tolerant than others of wet or dirty diapers. It is important that all children have this area of their bodies touched in *loving, matter-of-fact, and nonsexual ways* so that they learn about the acceptability of their genitalia. Touching a child in a sexually stimulating way is always wrong.

If you suspect abuse of any kind, find a way to protect your child. Get help if you need it.

Report the abuser to the child protection service in your area. See **Where to Go for Additional Help.**

—Christine Ternand, M.D.

Affirmations for Growth

Affirmations are all the things that parents do and say that let children know that they are lovable and capable. The support, care, protection, and love that parents give help children accomplish the developmental tasks of the stage they are in.

An important emotional and social task of infants is to learn to trust, to decide to be. They need to experience and to be sure that it is all right for them to live, to be who they are, to have needs, and to find ways to get those needs met. Babies reach out with eyes, voices, and wiggles to the people in their world, and their most important people are you, the parents. When they trust (bond with) their parents, they can learn to trust their world. Babies need to hear these messages.

Affirmations for Being

• I'm glad you are alive.
• You belong here.
• What you need is important to me.
• I'm glad you are you.
• You can grow at your own pace.
• You can feel all of your feelings.
• I love you, and I care for you willingly.

You give these positive messages by the way you respond to, hold, look at, talk to, and care for your baby. Saying the affirmations or singing them several times a day reminds you to express them through your care, and babies often respond to your voice with serious alertness or calmness.

Of course, you have to believe the affirmations in order for them to be effective. Otherwise you offer conflicting messages that confuse children. Infants who believe that their adults mean these lifegiving messages are encouraged to grow and to be about the important task of learning to trust their environment and themselves.

You can read more about what affirmations mean and don't mean and how to use them in families in Clarke's *Self-Esteem: A Family Affair*. The affirmations are adapted from Pamela Levin's *Becoming the Way We Are*. (See **Resources**.)

—Jean Illsley Clarke

Parents Get Another Chance—
Recycling

Not only are parents of infants taking care of their babies, but they, like children, have developmental tasks to accomplish. In her book, *Becoming the Way We Are*, Pamela Levin explains a way of thinking about those tasks, the theory of recycling.

What Is Recycling?

The theory of recycling notes that adults go through a cyclical growth process, often without noticing it, in which they refocus on earlier developmental tasks. Parents are triggered to recycle whatever stage their children are in, so parents of infants often upgrade or polish their ability to trust and to be.

Recycling Being Tasks

Parents who are taking care of a new baby have the opportunity to rethink and feel their own BEING and dependency needs.

They may experience a wish to withdraw from the demands of the outside world. Moms and Dads at home may long for someone to take care of them. Dads or Moms at work may find themselves daydreaming about the baby and wondering what is going on at home. Or they may simply experience a heightened emotional state: "I don't know why I've been feeling so touchy lately," they may say, or, "I feel good about the whole world today!"

Many Moms report that they are acutely alert to the needs of their babies, while their thinking about other things feels "mushy" and that they are less interested in getting back to work outside the home than they had thought they would be.

Parents who didn't get the Being affirmations (see page 14) the first time around can take them now as they offer them to their children.

You can say them to yourself like this:

- I'm glad I'm alive.
- I'm glad I'm a woman/man.
- I can grow at my own pace. I don't have to be a perfect parent, only willing to learn.
- I am lovable.
- My needs are important.

Parents during this stage need to receive care and nurturing from other adults and should arrange to get all the support that they can. The needs of the parents are often overlooked both by the parents themselves and by anyone else who could serve as their caretaker because of the infant's newness and needs.

Parents need to be nurtured. Their needs are

- to be held (getting lots of hugs),
- to be fed (having meals prepared),
- to get rest (lots of sleep to support lots of baby and family changes),
- to have a clean environment (bedroom, bathroom, laundry, kitchen),

- to hear positive messages ("I'm so glad to see you and talk with you." "What a wonderful mother/father you are!"),
- to be shown concern ("Tell me about your day." "How was your night last night?"),
- to get support for their parenting skills (*not*, "They never did it that way in my day."),
- a source of accurate parenting information, and
- time alone together to renew themselves and their relationship. This is essential and not a luxury.

To recognize these needs and get them met is vitally important to the parents and also to the welfare of the next generation: their baby. As partners in this endeavor, parents can get some of these needs met by each other; however, having outside support people to help is very important. One doctor we know writes prescriptions for help that Moms and Dads can present to their closest support persons.

Remember: A truly fulfilled parent is indeed the best parent available!

—Jean Illsley Clarke and Samara Kemp

A. Crying

My baby cries and fusses. What do I do?

- Start infant massage every day for about one half-hour.
- Bundle her, hold her close, and take a walk outside.
- Warm a blanket in a 150-degree oven for her.
- Hold her over your shoulder and keep moving.
- Tape record her own cry and play it back. Try it!
- Put her in a Snugli or back carrier.
- Take a shower or bath with her.
- Rock and sing to her. It helps both mother and child to relax.
- Go for a car or stroller ride.
- I do relaxation techniques for myself, like yoga, massage, meditation, and imagining her quiet, comfortable, happy.
- Cut out stimulation like TV, lights, toys.
- Help her find her fist to suck.
- Take off her clothes, then let her lie on her back and kick.
- Touch her with calm, confident hands.
- Rhythmic movement helps—swinging, rocking, dancing, walking.
- Wrap her in a blanket and lay her on the dryer. The heat and warmth and sound may be soothing. Stay close to hold her there safely.
- Try an infant swing.

(See also A-2, A-5, D-1, I-3, and **Ages and Stages**.)

Thanks to Ellen Peterson, Circle from Concord, California

My colicky two-month-old cries for more than an hour at a time and cannot be comforted. Why does he cry like this and what do I do?

- He cries because he is in pain. He is distressed.
- It could be gas. Lift his knees and push them gently against his chest.
- He could have what is called an "immature" digestive or nervous system. Hang in with him until he grows out of it.
- Keep track of your diet and see if certain foods you eat cause your baby to cry six- to twenty-four hours later if you are nursing.
- Ask your physician. Listen to her assessment.
- The baby may be wound up and tired.
- Put him in bed for ten to fifteen minutes and then try comforting him again.
- Do everything gentle and nurturing you can think of. You may never know why he cries.
- Stay with him, rocking, singing, or just holding him so he knows he is not alone in his misery.
- Get help from someone else.
- Don't look at it as your failure.
- Offer extra feedings if he wants them.
- Don't let yourself get beyond control. Take breaks when you need to.

(See also A-1, A-7, and **Parents Get Another Chance—Recycling**.)

Thanks to Ellen Peterson, Circle from Lafayette, California

My baby is fussing. How do I know if she's teething and what do I do?

- When babies are teething, they chew on their lips or bite things.
- Give her a cold, wet washcloth to chew on. If it comforts her, she may be teething.
- She may arch her back a lot if she's teething.
- Feel her gums to see if they are taut like a blister. They will look white before the tooth breaks through.
- Wrap an ice cube in a washcloth and let her chew on it.
- Offer safe things to gnaw on, like toys and measuring spoons.
- Try the special teething rings that are fluid filled and can be frozen.
- See if her gums feel tighter and harder.
- Let her chew on crushed ice tied in cheese cloth.

Thanks to Darlene Mortz, Circle from Yakima, Washington

My three-month-old screams for over an hour whenever he's left with anyone but me. I seem to be the only one who can comfort him.

- Whenever the sitter is holding or feeding him make sure the same music is playing and she is wearing the same robe or cologne you wear when you feed him.
- Arrange to work in your home and have the care provider there so the baby can see you.
- Give it time. He'll outgrow it.
- Let him be in lots of people's arms.
- A mother and child have a real special relationship at three months. It is not a good time to introduce a new person. Accept the situation for now, and try again in a month or two.
- Tell the baby, "You are OK," while he is with someone else. Say, "You are fed and are in good hands."
- Tell the baby that it is OK to cry.
- Enjoy the reward of being the one who can soothe him.
- Help him use a "blankie" or "lovey" that he can hold when you are gone.
- Try another care provider with a new style.
- Stay home more and have people come to you for now.

(See also I-2.)

Thanks to Ellen Peterson, Circle from Lafayette, California

My baby is fine all day but has a crying spell for three or four hours in the evening. What can I do?

- Know that babies generally have a fussy period each day and that evening is a typical time.
- Some tiny babies like to be swaddled—that is, wrapped snugly in a blanket.
- Take turns with your partner during the fussy time.
- See if taking a bath with the baby helps.
- Dance around to music. It may help her to burp!
- Lie down on your bed. Put a warm water-bottle or heating pad (set on low) on your belly, and then settle your baby on top, tummy down.
- Give yourself a nice evening away each week. It's OK to get a sitter for a crying baby.
- Play classical music while you stroke her softly.
- Talk to her; use your voice to soothe her.
- Take her for a ride in the car in an approved car seat.
- Put her in a swing and swing her and sing to her.
- Plan your schedule to have time to devote to the baby during fussy periods.

(See also A-1, A-2, A-7, F-9.)

Thanks to Ellen Peterson, Circle from Alamo, California

Are you spoiling a baby if you pick him up every time he cries?

• No, he needs to be held.
• Babies are not mean. If you tend to them now, they'll trust you and cry less later.
• "Spoiling" is an idea forty years out of date.
• Let him entertain himself in gradually increasing amounts of time.
• It is unnatural for a baby to be away from his mother when he wants to be close.
• No, yet you need to get other things done, too.
• Doctors say you can't spoil an infant.
• Crying isn't "good" for babies, even though many of our parents were taught it was.
• This is his only way to call for you. He can't talk yet.
• Avoid always picking him up in anticipation of his needs. Sometimes, when he cries, pick him up immediately so he will learn that you care. Other times, let him come to a full cry and then respond immediately, so he will learn he can call out to get his needs met.

(See also A-7, A-8, D-9, and **Ages and Stages**.)

Thanks to Ellen Peterson, Circle from Lafayette, California

How long should we let our baby cry?

• Respond right away.
• Not long.
• Trust your instincts and feelings each time.
• Not more than fifteen minutes before you comfort her. She may cry long after that but do hold, talk to, or attend to her.
• Check for pins, wet diapers, etc., then trust your feelings.
• Watch to see if your baby cries at predictable times. Arrange your schedule so you can respond quickly and give time to the baby then.
• Until the song or the music box is over.
• I think five minutes is enough.
• Some babies need to cry ten minutes or more before sleep. It won't hurt your baby to try this.
• Learn to recognize your baby's different cries and what each one means. Use this knowledge as a guide in each situation.
• Respond after the baby comes to a full cry.

(See also A-6, A-8.)

Thanks to Ellen Peterson, Circle from Berkeley, California

When do we start discipline? I feel like my six-month-old has us wrapped around his finger. Whenever I leave the room, he fusses and cries. What should I do?

• Discipline begins early. When your infant hurts you—by pulling your hair, grasping, or biting your breast—teach him that it is not OK by gently removing whatever he's hurting.
• Stay in the room within eyesight.
• Take him with you.
• Call to him. Let him know you're there when you leave the room.
• A baby is not mature enough to know you will return when you leave a room. Get him interested in a toy or music box before you go.
• Remember that *discipline* means "to teach." Think about what you want to teach him. Discipline is not punishment.
• Fussing when you leave the room is OK for a short while. Congratulate yourself that your baby has bonded well with you and is "checking in." You have things you need to do; do them.
• Make sure he is in a safe place before you leave any room.
• Are you sacrificing yourself for him at every turn? Babies will adjust to family needs and patterns. You're the adult. Take charge.

(See also A-1, A-6, A-7, I-2, **Ages and Stages**, and **About Abuse and Neglect**.)

Thanks to Ellen Peterson, Circle from Lafayette, California

When my child cries, I want to shake her. My physician says this can cause brain damage. What can I do with my anger that won't hurt anyone?

- Get relief immediately for yourself. Put your baby down and stomp on the floor in another room, or shake a pillow instead.
- Let someone else take over for a while.
- Call Parents Anonymous in your area.
- Set your baby down in a crib or safe place and call a neighbor or friend for help.
- Yell (someplace away from the baby).
- Do some deep breathing and center yourself.
- Cry.
- Count to ten.
- Turn energy into action: shoot baskets, clean the house, go for a walk, pull weeds, etc.
- Get support from your friends.
- Get more rest.
- Get some counseling to find out the root causes of your impatience.

(See also F-1, **About Abuse and Neglect**, and **Parents Get Another Chance—Recycling**.)

Thanks to Ellen Peterson, Circle from Lafayette, California

B. Breast- and Bottle-feeding

How can my newborn be hungry? I just fed him less than two-and-one-half hours ago. Should I feed him again?

- He's really tiny. So is his tummy.
- A newborn's tummy is the size of his fist. It needs to be filled often.
- Check and make sure your milk is in and lets down before he feeds.
- Yup.
- I'd do it.
- Offer to feed him.
- If you are nursing, try to keep feeding times two or more hours apart to avoid breast problems.
- Go ahead. He will extend the times soon. Remember, in the womb he had a constant food supply.
- Trust your intuition about yourself and your baby.
- Sure.
- Throw away your watch.
- He's just getting himself arranged. Offer a pacifier or finger for sucking first. If it's not just a sucking need, offer food.
- Are you sure the child is hungry when he cries? Go through your checklist of what a newborn would cry for.

(See also B-4, B-5.)

Thanks to Gail Davenport, Circle from Alderwood Manor, Washington

Where can I get help with breast-feeding problems?

• A hospital's postpartum floor.
• Your YWCA or YMCA may offer infant care classes.
• Childbirth education classes.
• Other breast-feeding parents.
• The La Leche League or other lactation consultants.
• Your doctor or nurse practitioner. Any time you take drugs, get your doctor's OK because some drugs concentrate in the milk. Drugs that are helpful to adults may be harmful to babies.
• Friends who have successfully breast-fed.
• Books on nutrition and breast-feeding. (See **Resources**.)
• Midwives.

Thanks to Samara Kemp, Circle from Ceres, California

What do you do with a baby who is bottle-feeding and doesn't want to stay in your arms?

- Sounds like he's finished. I take my baby's cues. I just say, "No more? OK."
- Be aware of the moods of your child, and feed him when he is calm.
- Have someone else feed the baby at times. See if he settles in better, and note how that person holds him.
- See if feeding in a quiet, darkened room, free of most distractions helps.
- Don't prop the bottle! Lay him down next to you and hold the bottle.
- Make sure your arms are safe and protective and are not suffocating or squeezing the child.
- Let your baby feed in a way preferable to him.
- Let go of doing it a certain way. Be flexible.
- Nestle with him in the corner of the couch, chair, bed—whatever.
- Let him lie down and take the bottle. Keep touching, patting, or caressing him.
- Lie down next to the child. Talk and touch him. Be responsive; sing; maintain intimacy, while feeding in whatever ways you find comfortable.
- Give him lots of cuddling, hugs, and holding at other times.

Thanks to Samara Kemp, Circle from Turlock, California

How long should I breast-feed if it's frustrating to the whole family?

- Have each person take responsibility for his own frustration. Talk about it together. Then decide.
- Depends on your patience level.
- How important is it to you to nurse? Resolve this first.
- Stop now if you don't really want to continue nursing.
- For three months. That way, you will have time to get your milk established and work out the kinks. Then decide what you want to do about it.
- Not long.
- Determine what's frustrating, the nursing or the demands on your time to do other things, and then decide what you want to change.
- You may need the support of your husband to accomplish this task. You should each voice your views of nursing to find out if you have some negative attitudes that affect your ability to nurse the baby. Then decide.

(See Ages and Stages and Affirmations for Growth.)

Thanks to Samara Kemp, Circle from Lafayette, California

How do I know if my baby is getting enough milk?

• Check with your doctor.

• If he sleeps well and gains weight, he is getting enough.

• If he spits the nipple out, he has enough for now.

• From time to time, babies require more milk to grow. Feed your baby whenever he wants to eat.

• If the baby is growing and seems contented, he is getting enough.

• When he's done, burp him and offer the breast or bottle again. If he refuses, he's had enough.

• If the baby is losing weight or not gaining weight, he isn't getting enough.

• If the baby cries a lot, ask your doctor to see if he is having an allergic reaction to the milk.

• Plenty of wet diapers? Ask your doctor how often your baby should be urinating.

• Throw away your watch and feed him whenever he wishes.

(See also B-1.)

Thanks to Gail Nordeman, Circle from Healdsburg, California

My baby throws up after feeding. What should I do?

- Call your doctor or nurse and describe exactly what happens. Note especially how much is thrown up, how long after the feeding it happens, and how strongly the vomit is ejected. Follow the instructions.
- In addition to calling your doctor, call a La Leche League counselor with the same information.
- Burp her several times *during* a feeding, as well as after.
- See if it helps to feed her before she cries hard and swallows a lot of air.
- Lay her over your knees or high on your shoulder to "press" air up.
- Avoid juggling, swinging, or playing with her right after feedings.
- Some babies gulp in a lot of air as they feed; help them get the air up any way that works.
- Try burping her by rubbing her back while holding her in the "clam" position—sitting, doubled over so her head is close to her toes.
- If she's bottle-fed, consider trying another formula, but check first with your doctor.
- Watch your baby's weight-gain chart. If she's gaining according to her "norms" don't worry.
- Try having her sleep on her tummy, and raise the head of the bed a bit.

(See also B-1.)

Thanks to Ellen Peterson, Circle from Walnut Creek, California

I want to express my own milk rather than use a formula, but I am getting little milk. What should I do?

• Say to yourself as you pump or express, "My baby will benefit from this milk."

• Picture the baby in your mind when you express or pump.

• Massage yourself first to encourage the let-down reflex.

• First take a warm shower or apply a warm washcloth to your breasts to encourage milk flow.

• Have someone show you how on your breast or hers. I couldn't learn from descriptions in a book.

• Expressing breast milk is a learned skill that takes practice. Save whatever amount you get in the freezer and add to it until you get several ounces.

• Get a good pump, not just a bulb type. Rent an electric one.

• Call a La Leche League counselor in your area.

• For manual expression, press gently, firmly, and in a radial motion around the breast and the brown area around the nipple.

• Borrow pumps from friends. Some breasts work best with one pump, some with another, and some don't work with any pumps.

• Take your time until you get the hang of it.

(See also B-2.)

Thanks to Sandy Sittko, Circle from St. Louis, Missouri

When should I start "solid food"?

- Four to six months of age or after is the current recommendation of the American Academy of Pediatrics.
- When your doctor recommends it.
- When your baby lets you know—she's not gaining weight—that she isn't getting enough calories. Even then, more milk may be the best answer.
- After six months, make your own baby food.
- Don't start because of pressure from grandparents or friends.
- Remember, even the experts disagree on this subject.
- When your baby sticks her fist in your food and sucks it off for herself.
- Read as much as you can on the subject, both "pro" and "con," before you decide.
- When you can't stand to eat in front of your baby and not share!
- Keep your own nutritional levels high, and breast-feed your baby as long as possible.

Thanks to Gail Nordeman, Circle from Healdsburg, California

How do you move a breast-fed baby to a bottle?

• Replace one breast-feeding a day, starting with the late morning feeding. After several days, replace the afternoon feeding and continue until all feedings are replaced with the bottle.

• Try different sterilized nipples. Old ones are good. Borrow them from friends.

• Make sure you hold your baby in the regular close position.

• Offer the bottle when the baby is sleepy.

• Offer the bottle when you are walking around and carrying her.

• Warm the milk to body temperature.

• Get your doctor's recommendation on what formula to use.

• Put expressed breast milk in the bottle.

• Take your time.

• Have someone else feed the baby. She can smell your milk if you offer the bottle, and she may refuse to take it from a bottle.

• Give her the bottle after you've nursed her, when she is not so frantic. Slip the nipple in her mouth.

(See also B-7.)

Thanks to Ellen Peterson, Circle from Lafayette, California

C. Sleeping

When will my baby sleep through the night?

- When the baby is ready. Tell her, "You don't have to hurry. You can take your time and sleep on your own schedule."
- When you stop getting anxious about it.
- Maybe never. Babies wake for different reasons throughout infancy and childhood.
- Depends on the baby's development and the parents' stress level.
- When you take the baby to bed with you.
- When you least expect it. The night that you wake up out of habit and lie there listening!
- Some people think it depends on the baby's weight.
- When the baby is no longer hungry during the night. You may have to delay responding to see if she can go back to sleep on her own.
- My baby slept through the night after I took the wool and feathers out of her room. She was allergic to them.

(See also C-4, C-5, C-6.)

Thanks to Ellen Peterson, Circle from Sonoma, California

Our baby was sleeping through the night and now is waking up two or three times a night. I feel tense and a little crazy! What can I do?

- Check to see that he is OK. Then, go back to bed, and breathe deeply.
- Keep a journal of why and when he awakes.
- Pick him up, snuggle him, then put him down and pat his back.
- Let your mate hold the baby when you are tense, because babies pick up the tension, cry more themselves, and then create more tension for everyone.
- Set a time limit for letting him cry. For example, wind up a toy and when it stops playing, pick up the baby.
- Analyze what's changed in his life.
- Think ahead of time and agree as a couple on what you will do in the middle of the night.
- Take the baby to bed with you. Say, "I love you. Your needs are OK. I'm here for you."
- Go ahead and feed him if he is hungry.
- Accept that he needs to wake up right now. Get some sleep during the daytime.
- Get in touch with your own feelings and see a counselor about feeling crazy.
- See yourself getting more rest: naps, earlier bedtime, weekend sleep-ins. Then do it.

(See also A-7, C-5.)

Thanks to Ellen Peterson, Circle from Orinda, California

Our three-month-old is sleeping in our room. When and how should I move her out? The baby's room is too far away from ours for us to hear her when she cries at night.

- In some cultures, whole families sleep in the same room. Think and feel what will be right for you.
- Dr. Spock says six months is a good age to move her. (See **Resources**.)
- Leave the baby in your room as long as you want to and find someplace else to make love.
- Buy an intercom so you can hear your baby in her room. You can plug it into any room and use it during naps, too!
- When our baby was four days old, we moved her out. When she needs me, she really yells. I don't wake with the little noises, and she doesn't wake with ours.
- Consider rearranging sleeping rooms so the baby can be nearer your room or you can be nearer to her.
- Move her out gradually—just outside the door first, then down the hall, then farther away, etc.

Thanks to Ellen Peterson, Circle from Sonoma, California

42

My baby has day and night mixed up. What can I do?

- Make sure the baby's needs for contact are met during the day so he doesn't stay up at night.
- Check the lighting and shading. Have lots of light during the day and no light at night. Same for noise—eliminate sudden noises at night.
- See that the baby isn't overstimulated during the day, causing him to stay awake at night.
- Gradually bring your baby's schedule forward by waking him up during his daytime nap so he'll go to sleep earlier in the evening. Take about two weeks to do it and be consistent with what you do every day. Brazelton explains how in *Infants and Mothers*. (See **Resources**.)
- Give the baby his bath in the late evening, then feed him and put him to bed.
- Read *Crying Babies, Sleepless Nights*, by Sandy Jones. (See **Resources**.)
- Experiment with letting him cry himself to sleep for ten minutes. Some babies seem to get *more* stimulated when picked up.
- Offer light feeding and light stimulation—holding, talking—before bedtime.
- Many babies need at least three weeks to adjust after those long, dark months in the womb.
- Curl up in bed with him when he *does* sleep. Get some sleep yourself.

(See also C-1, C-2, C-5.)

Thanks to Gail Nordeman, Circle from Healdsburg, California

My baby's naps are so irregular, I can't make any plans. How can I get her on a schedule?

- The baby *is* on her schedule. Listen to the rhythm of the baby and adjust *your* schedule.

- Keep a record for seven days of when she sleeps and eats. To discover her pattern, divide a paper into half-hour segments and jot down what she is doing.

- Remember that in the early months a baby's schedule changes every few days. In *Your Baby & Child* Penelope Leach describes this period as "unsettled." (See **Resources**.) As she matures, her schedule will become more predictable.

- Bathe and feed her right before you want her to sleep for a longer period. Do this at the same time every day.

- Don't try to schedule her right now. Treat yourself to a babysitter a couple afternoons a week and use that time to get things done.

- Gradually change her schedule by taking the baby into an environment that is stimulating during the time you want her awake.

- Don't. This is an opportunity to quiet your life and break from the hectic pace of the world.

- Go ahead and make plans. Adjust them later if you need to. Think positive!

(See also C-1, C-4, F-9, **Ages and Stages**, and **Parents Get Another Chance—Recycling**.)

Thanks to Jean Clarke, Circle from Minneapolis, Minnesota

How can I get enough rest and sleep?

• Remember, you will get more sleep as the baby gets older. In the meantime, sleep when the baby sleeps.

• Rearrange your priorities and be more insistent with your husband about your needs. Ask for his help.

• Program yourself. Unplug the phone, put a note on the door, and nap when the baby sleeps.

• Practice good eating habits. Exercise, too!

• Let the house go and rest. Get a cleaning helper.

• Have Dad father the baby while you rest.

• Lie down for ten minutes out of every hour.

• Your baby and you need quantity and quality time. Don't shortchange yourselves: you can't live this time over again. Enjoy the baby and let others cook and pamper you.

• Don't pick up the baby every time he whimpers. Let the child come to a full cry first.

• Accept offers and ask for help from friends and relatives.

• Nurse your baby in bed. Relax and enjoy this age.

• Don't be a Super Mom. Be real and recognize your own needs too.

(See also F-7, F-10, I-7, and **Parents Get Another Chance—Recycling**.)

Thanks to Samara Kemp, Circle from Modesto, California

D. Bonding and Growth

What is this bonding everyone talks about?

- Bonding is an attachment to the baby that continues throughout life.
- Bonding is a relationship based on an exchange through sensory experiences (i.e., holding, feeding, loving) between parent and child.
- Bonding is a psychological connection between the parents and the baby.
- It is the protective feelings of the parents and the infant's preference for his parents.
- Bonding is what babies need to grow and trust. Babies need parents who are willing to bond.
- It is nature's way of ensuring our survival.
- Bonding is an inherent desire to care for and connect with your baby.
- The invisible glue that keeps you close.
- It is the need for close physical and emotional contact with the baby, the desire to touch, look at, and respond to the baby's cry.
- It is reflecting your baby's smile so you and the baby feel connected.
- Read Polly Berends's highly inspirational chapter, "Wholeness," in *Whole Child/Whole Parent* for a beautiful perspective on connectedness. (See **Resources**.)

(See also D-2, H-3, **Ages and Stages**, and **Affirmations for Growth**.)

Thanks to Ellen Peterson, Circle from Lafayette, California

When should bonding happen?

- Bonding is a process that begins the moment your baby is born and continues from birth to five years.
- I think it happens before birth because even in utero, the baby shows his own style as he and Mom learn to live together.
- When you hear your baby cry, you begin bonding.
- The process begins from birth. Hold and touch your baby from the beginning. If you don't feel it right away, don't worry. The feeling will come.
- When you see the baby and look into the baby's eyes.
- From day one.
- It starts WHENEVER—for me, in utero.
- Right after birth unless a cesarean has been performed under general anesthesia. Then, as soon as Mom feels she is ready.
- It's life-long! There is no one, magic moment.
- Before birth.
- At birth.
- With some, it is during pregnancy. With others, it doesn't happen until the baby smiles and responds, or when the parent relaxes.

(See also D-3.)

Thanks to Samara Kemp, Circle from Sacramento, California

How can you tell that bonding is happening?

• When your baby is responsive to you and affected by your actions.

• When your baby smiles when she sees you. When your baby cries and you feel protective toward her.

• When you notice how much time you spend thinking about your baby.

• Bonding is a process, so it doesn't happen instantly. When you become more involved with your child day after day and you feel an overwhelming desire to care for and be with your baby, you are bonding.

• Klaus and Kennell describe it in *Bonding: The Beginnings of Parent-Infant Attachment*. (See **Resources**.)

• When you feel that surge of love.

• When your baby shows he doesn't like you to be far away.

• T. Berry Brazelton says that stages of bonding take four months to complete. (See **Resources**.)

• Burton White says it takes three years to create a strong bond. (See **Resources**.)

• When you are giving and believing the affirmations for growth, you are bonding. (See **Affirmations for Growth**, page 14.)

(See also D-2 and **Parents Get Another Chance—Recycling**.)

Thanks to Ellen Peterson, Circle from Lafayette, California

Should we take our three-month-old infant on our four-day anniversary trip or leave her with Grandma? What would you do?

- Take her. I wouldn't want to leave my baby with anyone else.
- When you need to get away, go out to dinner instead and plan a trip away from her when she is older.
- Your needs are important and so are the baby's.
- Go two days with her and two days without her.
- Take her. We had fun having our baby along on a similar trip.
- Listen to your inner feelings and then make your decision.
- Take her. Four days is very long, and parents and babies belong together.
- Only leave her with someone she is used to seeing every day and who already has a strong relationship established with her.
- Take a caretaker along with you so you can get out and still have daily contact with your baby.

(See also I-3 and **Ages and Stages**.)

Thanks to Ellen Peterson, Circle from Lafayette, California

I've heard so much about infant stimulation. What is it? What do I do?

• It is supporting her need to know and grow *at her own pace, in her own way.*

• Offer something for all her senses—music, mirrors, massage with oils, laughter, lullabies, and your skin.

• Try an unbreakable mirror in the crib.

• Smile.

• Offer safe things to touch and taste.

• Talk to her a lot. Call her by name.

• Listen to her sounds and repeat them back to her.

• Before you decide to use a stimulation program, watch to see what kind of stimulation she responds to. Also, how much does she like?

• The trend today is to overstimulate. Enjoy your child instead.

• Hold her and give lots of loving touch. Learn about infant massage in books or a class.

• Use a ready-made infant stimulation program only if you have trouble holding, touching, and interacting with your baby.

• Read *Infant Toddler: The Joy of Learning*, by Earladeen Badger. (See **Resources**.)

• If you bombard her with sensory experiences, she may get frustrated, because you are pushing her.

(See also **Ages and Stages** and **About Abuse and Neglect**.)

Thanks to Gail Nordeman, Circle from Healdsburg, California

My five-month-old isn't turning over yet and his cousin, who's the same age, is. How can I stimulate him to turn over?

• Don't worry about it. Let them grow at their own speeds. Enjoy what they do.
• Know that your baby is the star in your heart.
• Babies do things at different rates. Timing is different for each one. Let him play on a blanket on the floor, where he'll have rooom to stretch and strengthen his muscles.
• Babies do things different ways. Some wait a long time and then surprise you by doing a new task very well the first time.
• Sounds like unhealthy parental competition. Let him be on his own time clock.
• Don't. Let your baby roll over when he wants to.
• Refer to a good book on child development.
• Read Bob Greene's *Good Morning, Merry Sunshine* for one father's feelings about experiences during the first year. (See **Resources**.)
• Read *Infants and Mothers*, by T. Berry Brazelton—it reports on the development of three different babies. (See **Resources**.)
• This could be a sign of family competition. Don't act it out through your babies.

(See also D-7 and **Ages and Stages**.)

Thanks to Ellen Peterson, Circle from Lafayette, California

My baby isn't at all like I expected her to be! Help!

- Hold your baby and look at her. Touch her often when you're not physically caring for her. It takes time to get to know one another.
- Let her grow on you.
- Close your eyes and just listen to her a while.
- Your child may experience you as different, too. Take your time.
- You have already spent nine months together; draw on that.
- Don't feel guilty. Accept your feelings and take time to see your baby in other ways.
- Discover what it is about this baby you *do* like and write these things down.
- Everybody has a fantasy of what baby will be like. You will adjust your expectations as you accept what is.
- Examine your feelings without judgment. Let go of your imaginings.
- In *Between Generations*, Ellen Galinsky reports that accepting "this baby" is a common task for new parents. (See **Resources**.)
- The more you love your baby, the better she will seem to you. Loving takes time.
- You can't control everything. Instead, enjoy your baby and thank her for being who she is.

(See also D-1, D-2, and **Affirmations for Growth**.)

Thanks to Gail Nordeman, Circle from Healdsburg, California

I am concerned that my baby's father doesn't hold our baby close and only engages in "rough" play. I want to encourage them to develop a close, nurturing relationship. What can I do?

• Tell Dad how you feel. Find out how he feels about the baby and what kind of relationship he wants with him. Ask him how you can help.

• Ask him to give a bottle to the baby.

• Agree on a time they will spend alone together.

• Have Dad take over in the evenings.

• Play is an OK way to be close.

• He may feel insecure. Ask him if he wants you to show him how to snuggle and cuddle the baby.

• Build up his confidence by commenting in a positive way when he nurtures you or the baby.

• If you are concerned about your baby's safety, intervene. If not, enjoy their playing.

• Get lots of different kinds of books—some about playing, stimulation, development, etc. Learn together what is "normal." (See **Resources**.)

• Recent research shows that males and females play differently with babies and that babies as young as one week old respond differently to a man or to a woman entering the room. Enjoy the difference.

(See also F-12, **Affirmations for Growth, Ages and Stages**, and **About Abuse and Neglect**.)

Thanks to Ellen Peterson, Circle from Sonoma, California

Is my baby getting enough love or too much? How do I know?

- Babies are very sensitive to feelings, and they get their first impressions of the world through them. Take good care of yourself so you can show lots of love to your baby.
- No, babies don't get too much love.
- In *Babyhood*, Penelope Leach says you can't spoil a child under six months old. (See **Resources**.)
- If your baby is healthy and smiles at you, he is getting enough.
- There cannot be too much love, but there could be smothering. If you want to read about this, see Clarke's *Self-Esteem: A Family Affair*. Smother-love is called marshmallowing in that book. (See **Resources**.)
- If he is developing well physically and learning to trust, he is getting enough love.
- A baby who is not responding may not be getting enough attention.
- One way to ensure enough love is to say the affirmations and act upon them every day. (See page 14.)
- Take time to feel the love you share with your baby. Hear it and smell it.

(See also A-6, **Ages and Stages**, **Affirmations for Growth**, and **Parents Get Another Chance—Recycling**.)

Thanks to Samara Kemp, Circle from Lafayette, California

My infant is five months old. How long should I let him use a pacifier?

- Watch the baby and see when he decides he doesn't need it anymore.
- Until he has his first few teeth.
- Let him use it until he wants to stop.
- It is easier later to remove the pacifier than the thumb. So continue as long as he wants it.
- GRADUALLY limit the times and places it is OK for him to suck on the pacifier. Let him have it when he goes to sleep if he fusses for it then.
- Let him throw it away himself.
- Many children lose interest as their sucking need declines. Introduce another sleeptime lovey like a quilt or stuffed animal while gradually limiting the use of the pacifier.
- Poke a hole in the pacifier when the baby is about two or two-and-a-half-years-old. Continue to let him suck it. He will soon lose interest because it will be less satisfying.

Thanks to Ellen Peterson, Circle from Pleasant Hill, California

E. Changes in Marriage

How will my marriage change now that we have a baby?

- Tremendously. This is the most dramatic change your relationship will see: going from two to three.
- Every marriage is different and unpredictable. Use this occasion to create what you want.
- The baby may trigger competition in the family. Make private time with each person, including yourself.
- Some couples become closer and much more intimate. Some couples have difficulty and move apart.
- You will need each other in different ways. If you listen to your needs, you both will grow.
- Your sexual feelings may be altered by the presence of a child in the house.
- You will probably become more mature and responsible.
- The demand for you to operate as a team will increase tremendously.
- You will have new expectations of each other in new roles.
- Babies take tremendous time and energy.
- You and your spouse may be recycling this stage, and you may need to be cared for yourself. (See page 16.)

(See also E-2, E-3, E-4, and **Parents Get Another Chance—Recycling**.)

Thanks to Gail Nordeman, Circle from Healdsburg, California

My husband is jealous of the attention I give to our baby. What can I do?

- Ask him what he needs to do about his jealousy. Then tell him to do it.
- Tell him about your concern.
- Encourage him to bottle-feed the baby to get some of that good intimacy with the baby for himself.
- Separate what part of this problem is yours and what is his.
- Remember, Moms and Dads need loving too.
- Give him Clarke's tape, *The Important Infants*, to listen to. (See **Resources**.)
- Set up special times together. Go for walks together with Dad carrying the baby in a pack.
- Spend some time each day pleasuring each other.
- Ask about his day and when he responds, really listen.
- You and he decide which chores you both can put aside for next year so you can spend more time together now.
- Leave the baby with a sitter, and go see a movie or go out for dinner. Hold hands.
- Encourage him to hold the baby a lot.
- Take a shower with him.
- Talk, yell, rant, and rave until he hears that you want him to stop this jealous stuff and help raise the child.

(See also E-3.)

Thanks to Ellen Peterson, Circle from Lafayette, California

How do you keep parenting from overwhelming your relationship with your spouse?

- Make time for the two of you.
- Use sitters regularly.
- Take the baby for a walk together and talk about each other, not the baby.
- Buy season tickets for something—the theater, sporting events, etc.—then use them.
- Choose your outings for the two of you—dinner together, for instance, instead of a party with other people.
- Make a conscious effort to talk about news, books, etc. One piece a day from the radio, a magazine, or neighbors.
- Stay up together after the baby is asleep.
- Each make a list of things you want to do with the other. Then practice the art of the possible.
- Both of you take care of your health, rest, and nutrition needs so you have energy for each other.
- Get sexy!

(See also E-2.)

Thanks to Ellen Peterson, Circle from Lafayette, California

Is there sex after babies? Help!

• Yes, cuddle a lot.
• Make sure you go out as a couple, without the baby, perhaps once a week.
• It's OK to say no to sex until you feel like it.
• Take the baby to a sitter's home so you two can be home together.
• Rent a hotel room for an afternoon.
• If you suspect a physical problem, check with your doctor.
• Rent an X-rated movie.
• Talk to other parents, especially ones with older kids.
• Listen to romantic music.
• Remain open to options of different times for making love. Make a date for 2:00 P.M. or 11:00 A.M.
• Use a lovely, fragrant massage oil.
• Have candlelight dinners.
• Share your intimacy desires.
• Play while being sexual.
• Explore other loving expressions.

Thanks to Ellen Peterson, Circle from Sonoma, California

Sex hurts! What to do?

- Get some vaginal jelly for lubrication.
- Call your doctor.
- Ask for lots of TLC from your husband.
- Spend more time on foreplay.
- Don't avoid sex. Experiment to find out what does feel good.
- Say no to intercourse. Do other sexy things.
- Go slowly.
- Maybe stitches are the problem. Fingers can gently stretch the vagina.
- If your fears are preventing pleasure, get counseling.
- Pay attention to the love being expressed by your mate.

(See also E-4.)

Thanks to Ellen Peterson, Circle from Lafayette, California

At what point is counseling in order for the marriage relationship?

• When there is no longer an understanding of each other or the ability to work through conflict.

• When one or both are not getting their needs met in the marriage.

• When you've lost contact with each other.

• When you long for something better for yourselves.

• As soon as you ask if it's necessary. Counseling can be with therapists, friends, pastors, parents, etc.

• When help is needed to solve problems.

• When you're not listening to each other.

• When one-on-one communication breaks down, impartial help can be valuable because the parents, as well as the baby, are "newborn" at this job and can use guidance in "their" growth.

• When one or both partners see that it is time.

• Whenever distress is evident and there is a willingness to improve the relationship.

• When someone is drinking too much or misusing other drugs.

• Whenever there is physical abuse.

Thanks to Samara Kemp, Circle from Turlock, California

My husband wants his wife home, doing the cooking and raising the kids, as in a traditional Italian family. I want to be out "in the world" and returning to school or work. What should I do to prevent a problem here?

• Read about how other mothers solve this problem in Kaye Lowman's *Of Cradles & Careers: A Guide to Reshaping Your Job to Include a Baby in Your Life*. (See **Resources**.)

• Remind him that a good mother takes care of herself as well as her baby and her husband.

• Consider part-time work or part-time school.

• Surprise him by playing the "traditional Italian Mama" occasionally.

• Help him understand that you and his mother are separate people. It's a different time and you have different needs.

• Consider staying home full-time while your child is young. You can return to work later, when your child is old enough for nursery or elementary school.

• Tell him your need to be out is not a reflection on his ability to provide.

• A recent survey showed that "at-home Moms" had higher stress levels than working Moms.

(See also E-6, F-9, and **Parents Get Another Chance—Recycling**.)

Thanks to Ellen Peterson, Circle from Sonoma, California

Now that the baby is here, my husband says he'll share the housework, but he doesn't do enough. What can I do?

- Do chores together.
- Listen to upbeat music to lighten and quicken the chores you share.
- Say, "This *needs* to be done. Do you want to do dinner or bathe the baby?"
- See if some of the chores can wait six months.
- Make a scene about this if that's what it takes to get his attention.
- Do less yourself.
- Make lists of chores on weekends, and decide on tasks. Divide the jobs by the days in the week; for example, one might prepare dinner every other day. Divide baby care by the times of the day.
- Be willing to teach him how to do housework and care for the baby.
- *Assume* he's going to share.
- Tell him to get off his duff and help!
- Enjoy the clean, finished work that you've done together.

(See also F-10, I-7.)

Thanks to Ellen Peterson, Circle from Lafayette, California

My spouse and I disagree about how to care for our baby, how long to let him cry, how to soothe him, how often to use a sitter, etc. What can we do?

- If you know more about it than your spouse does, teach your spouse.
- Negotiate on the sitter issue.
- Don't let your baby cry for more than fifteen minutes and find lots of ways to soothe him.
- It's OK to discover that your way isn't the only way! Sometimes my spouse's questions help me see another way.
- If both your ways are safe, each do it your way.
- Think. Solve problems; don't compete.
- If a safety issue is involved, ask your doctor for advice or call the police.
- Pick one topic, then each read something about it, talk to a parent of an older child you admire, compare notes, and decide on a way that pleases both of you.
- Keep your mouth shut while your spouse is learning something you already know.
- Agree to disagree.
- Take a parenting class together.

(See also A-1, A-5, A-7, E-6, F-13, **About Abuse and Neglect**, and **Where to Go for Additional Help**.)

Thanks to Samara Kemp, Circle from Lafayette, California

F. New Parents Have Needs, Too

Sometimes I lose patience and I don't think I should.

• It's OK to lose patience—get help. Ask for what you need.

• If you can, schedule a sitter daily and take a break.

• Lots of Moms fall into the "Madonna trap" and think they're not supposed to be human. Make a realistic list of what good mothers do or say. See Clarke's *Self-Esteem: A Family Affair* for an example. (See **Resources**.)

• Build in ways to get a break.

• Take a nap when your baby sleeps.

• At stressful times, turn to someone else to take over.

• Catch your feelings early and get help right away.

• It is natural to lose patience; it's what you do about it that matters.

• Keep one place in the house as your special spot and go there. Turn on soothing music for five to ten minutes to regain your composure.

• Forgive yourself. Accept yourself as human.

(See also A-7, A-9, C-6, D-1, **Affirmations for Growth, About Abuse and Neglect,** and **Parents Get Another Chance—Recycling.**)

Thanks to Ellen Peterson, Circle from Lafayette, California

How do I make new friends with other parents?

- By knowing you all have something wonderful in common and can share that.
- Ask the mail carrier if there are any babies in the neighborhood.
- Search for church- or city-sponsored "new moms" groups. Go.
- Listen for news of babysitting co-ops.
- Join exercise classes or take courses at school to meet people.
- Visit parenting classes, parent-participation activities, and nursery schools.
- Try the park on sunny mornings or the neighborhood pool on summer afternoons.
- Check community services and get involved.
- Baby stores and neighbors may serve as resources.
- Offer to babysit.
- Invite parents you meet to join you for a snack, a movie, or a stroller walk.
- Help someone else out.
- Photo studios are often full of new parents and their babies. Start a conversation with another parent.

(See also F-6, F-14.)

Thanks to Samara Kemp, Circle from Modesto, California

How can I maintain friendships with people who don't have children?

- Invite a childless friend to your house.
- Make time for yourself. Get a sitter so you'll have time for the friendship.
- Set a time in your mind on how much to talk "babies" and then focus on your friends and what they are interested in. Develop additional interests.
- Ask friends to bring food over and you'll provide the drinks.
- Tell friends that their friendship is important and ask them how you can work this out.
- Plan and schedule time together.
- If you are invited to do something with the baby, do it.
- Be willing to let go of some friendships and build new ones.
- Exercise together. Jog, workout, sauna, walk.
- Phone friends while folding diapers.
- Be open about your feelings and your needs.
- Ask for and get hugs!
- Get together for breakfast.

(See also F-14.)

Thanks to Ellen Peterson, Circle from Sonoma, California

Why are new mothers so forgetful, and how can I cope with my forgetfulness?

• Hormonal changes in the body affect the brain and allow emotions to run rampant. People often forget to do things that are not high priority.

• Nothing is as important as the baby. Other things slide past.

• Fatigue affects memory. Get more rest.

• Ask people to remind you of important things.

• Lots of Moms recycle this newborn stage and find that their thinking is baby-focused. Read *Self-Esteem: A Family Affair* to find out more. (See **Resources**.)

• Keep lists.

• Keep a calendar by the phone and write everything down.

• Use yellow stickems on the refrigerator and your mirror.

• Slow down.

• List your priorities each day and read the list several times during the day.

• I found Alan Lakein's *How to Get the Most Out of Your Time in Life* helpful in suggesting organizational skills. (See **Resources**.)

• Visualize a warm, bright candle clearing away the fog in your head.

(See **Parents Get Another Chance—Recycling**.)

Thanks to Ellen Peterson, Circle from Lafayette, California

How do I get back in shape?

- Check with your doctor first.
- Find a mother-baby exercise class.
- Watch an exercise program on TV. Gradually work up to full participation.
- Get an exercise record or tape. Invite another new mother to join you in doing the routine.
- Go for a walk every day for about a half-hour. Walk briskly and don't stop to "window shop" along the way.
- Take a yoga class.
- Keep track of your diet. Make sure you eat plenty of the nutritious foods. Keep junk foods and alcoholic drinks to a minimum. (No alcohol if you are nursing.)
- Plant a garden.
- Walk instead of driving to do short errands.
- Get Jane Fonda's book *Workout for Pregnancy, Birth, and Recovery*, and do the workout. (See **Resources**.)
- Organize a jogging co-op with other new mothers; rotate child care and runs.

(See also F-7.)

Thanks to Mary Paananen, Circle from Seattle, Washington

I'm the only one home on my block, and I feel so isolated. How do I deal with this loneliness?

• Call someone on the phone; listen to a friend for at least five minutes a day.

• Turn on the stereo and dance with your baby; sing.

• Attend an ongoing class with moms and babies, or form one that focuses on the needs of moms.

• Prearrange time for just the two of you with your mate.

• Look for an exercise class. Visit with others for a few minutes afterwards.

• Seek postpartum help service.

• Ask friends or relatives for what you need.

• Volunteer your talents to help others—for example, call an elderly person daily, work on a campaign, etc.

• Invite a mother you know to bring her child and meet you for a walk.

• Talk to people wherever you are.

• Treat yourself to a massage.

• Join a babysitting co-op.

• Ask people over.

(See also F-2, F-10.)

Thanks to Ellen Peterson, Circle from Walnut Creek, California

I feel I never have time for myself. What can I do about it?

• Tell your spouse you *need* it. Find some really good sitters or friends you can count on, even on the spur of the moment for emergencies. Trade babysitting services with them.

• *Take* time for yourself (it will not be given).

• When your baby is napping, do something you love to do.

• Take a class—exercise is great because you feel better. Have lunch with friends.

• Take five minutes of every hour for yourself.

• Leave the baby with a reliable person at least once a week and get out of the house, too. A child-care co-op is good for this.

• Cancel everything you can.

• *Take* time for yourself, you deserve and need it. Taking care of yourself is investing in the quality of the person who takes care of your baby.

• Do small things to love yourself—like drinking milk in a lovely stemmed glass, taking a bath with music and candlelight.

• Learn to use the moment. Do some deep breathing. Straighten your spine and feel a balance of body and mind with calm emotion. Read Gay Hendricks's *The Centering Book*. (See **Resources**.)

(See also C-6, F-8.)

Thanks to Samara Kemp, Circle from Sacramento, California

I loved the attention I received when I was pregnant. Now it's just the baby that people notice and fuss over. What about me?

• Fuss over yourself.
• Tell your close friends how you feel, and then ask them to talk about you part of the time.
• Join a parent-infant class to talk about how important your new role as a mother is.
• Do something pleasing for yourself—send yourself a balloon bouquet, have a massage, buy new shoes, get a manicure or haircut, prepare a childhood lunch treat.
• Write affirmations for yourself about your beautiful inner self.
• Post Mother's Day, Valentine, or birthday cards on your mirror. Read and believe them each day.
• Get your make-up done; buy new cologne.
• Get away; go out for an evening.
• Remember to say "thank you" and accept compliments for your baby and feel good about them yourself!
• Read parenting books to remind yourself that you are vitally important now.
• Read Leo Buscaglia's *Living, Loving and Learning*.

(See **Resources**.)

Thanks to Ellen Peterson, Circle from Lafayette, California

I have a two-month-old. I feel frustrated about not getting anything done. I have worked outside the home and am used to measuring the results at the end of each day.

• Say to yourself, "I'm doing what I'm supposed to be doing, and this is the most important thing I've ever done."

• Remember how fast infancy passes by. Some important careers show results long-term, not every day.

• You have kept another human being alive for one whole day. That is an accomplishment!

• Make that laundry pile disappear! Display those finished thank-you notes! Get praise!

• Divide projects into short segments. Cheer when you finish each part.

• Make a star chart. List all the jobs involved in keeping a two-month-old alive, and give yourself a star for each one you accomplish.

• Remember that your career will always be there but that your baby won't.

• Brag.

• Listen to Clarke's tape, *The Important Infants*, and don't be so hard on yourself. (See **Resources**.)

• Visit your old work place. Mine seemed nearly meaningless to me after I had been home with my baby.

(See also C-5.)

Thanks to Ellen Peterson, Circle from Oakland, California

I am asking the people in my family to care for me for the first time, but they're not used to giving me nurturing, especially my husband. What can I do?

- Ask your husband to say the affirmations to you once a day. (See page 14.) Then tell him what you need.
- Think about a specific thing you want. Ask for it. For example, say, "Will you bring out the old quilt and tuck it all around me?"
- Start with small requests they can succeed at. Thank them.
- Visualize them caring for you.
- Give and get massages.
- Ask to be held and cuddled. Explain that new moms need loving too. (Read about recycling, page 16.)
- Get lots of hugs from your spouse and family, and give them hugs every day.
- Be organized and divide household duties among family members. Stick to the plan. Don't do their jobs for them.
- Look for others who can nurture you: good friends, professionals, services for the home, sitters, etc.
- Look for nurturing in everything they do. When you find it, thank them.

(See also E-8, I-7, and **Parents Get Another Chance—Recycling**.)

Thanks to Ellen Peterson, Circle from Sonoma, California

I feel vulnerable about my baby. Everybody is telling me what to do, and I don't know how to stand up for myself.

- Talk to other mothers. Evaluate their experiences and decide for yourself.
- It's OK to tell people you want to think before you do what they tell you.
- Trust yourself and say affirmations to yourself.
- Ask yourself, "In this moment now, what feels right for me?"
- Think of your baby to reinforce your courage.
- Practice looking in the mirror while you tell them off!
- Write your beliefs down. Read them aloud.
- Get like a Momma bear and protect your cub!

Thanks to Ellen Peterson, Circle from Sonoma, California

What does "fathering" mean to you?

- Nurturing—same as "mothering."
- Concept should be "parenting"—either parent can care for a baby.
- Bonding with his child.
- It means "mothering minus breast-feeding": folding laundry, getting a snack for Mom while she nurses, etc.
- Honoring, respecting, and encouraging children.
- Getting to *really* know baby, not just doing tasks.
- Seeing your infant react to your attention.
- Sharing in the life of the child.
- It's not just raising a child, but also learning the idea of "family." The whole family needs to function.
- Being aware of the consequences of your actions.
- Having part of your mind and attention on someone else all the time.

(See also D-1, D-2, D-3.)

Thanks to Ellen Peterson, Circle from Lafayette, California

My wife wants me to help with our one-month-old son, but she criticizes me when I do. As a result, I don't want to help very much, and I feel guilty. What should I do?

• Decide what you feel is best, go ahead and do it.
• Take a parenting class together.
• Ask her to teach you about infant care.
• Forgive her; she may be unsure of herself in a new role.
• Look inside yourself. See your own ways of loving your son. Start there.
• You are *helping* with the baby, you are *fathering*. Do it.
• What may seem like criticism may be helpful. Listen for what you can use.
• Hand her a sheet of paper and tell her to list things for you to do, *with standards*.
• Pain produces change; act on it.
• Tell your wife that you feel criticized, and ask for two constructive suggestions for every criticism.
• Give her recognition for doing a competent job and being a loving mother. Ask for the same from her.
• Say, "Ouch, that hurts. New dads are tender, you know."
• Ask for positive, loving messages about your abilities.

(See also D-8, E-8, E-9, F-12, and **Affirmations for Growth**.)

Thanks to Deane Gradous, Circle from Minneapolis, Minnesota

How can I keep my brain alive with nobody to talk to all day but the baby?

- Study child development, and make a record of your baby's daily development.
- Take a course at your local Y, civic center, community college, or on television.
- Read some of the books you've always wanted to read.
- Get cassette tapes of intelligent people talking and listen to them.
- Take your baby to the park and talk to other mothers.
- Meditate.
- Get a baby carrier and take the baby with you to stimulating events.
- Start a book club.
- Invite a group of mothers and fathers to talk.
- Buy foreign language tapes and listen to them.
- Watch Donahue. Take a position. Share it.
- Take your baby to the library—read the front pages of two top newspapers.
- Play with a computer.
- Write poetry.
- Knit a complicated sweater or sew yourself a suit.

(See also F-2, F-6.)

Thanks to Gail Nordeman, Circle from Healdsburg, California

I get so tired of all this; sometimes I want to walk out the door and quit.

- Don't.
- Go out on the back step and scream. Then go back in the house and think about how to get some help.
- Phone a friend or call a neighbor over for a cup of coffee and a visit.
- Quit for an afternoon by having someone in to care for baby while you get out for a break.
- Care for your spiritual life.
- Babies are big commitments. Adjusting to family life involves lots of growing up. Hooray for you for doing it.
- It's common today to say, "Take this job and shove it." With babies, you may want to but don't do it.

(See also F-9, F-10.)

Thanks to Deane Gradous, Circle from Minnetonka, Minnesota

G. Grandparents

How do I tell my mother that I want to spend less time with her?

- By being very honest, and doing it gently and with kindness.
- You could tell her what you *do* need—positive things, like more time alone with your husband or baby.
- Tell her. Don't scold and don't hint. Be assertive about *your* needs, and tell her that you *do* care for her.
- Create a special time with her regularly and then explain that otherwise your schedule is busy and demanding.
- Gently, but firmly!
- Think about and decide how you *would* like to spend time with her.
- You are getting to know yourself, your baby, and your husband—just like a honeymoon—so you all need time to get adjusted. Ask your mother if she would please respect your new family needs.
- Put up a sign that says "Mother and baby are resting."
- I'd ask her to take the baby for the morning or the day. She'd have her grandchild and I'd have time to myself.
- Clearly, repeatedly, and lovingly.

Thanks to Samara Kemp, Circle from Modesto, California

How can I respond when my mother says, "You should do it this way," and my way is different?

- Do what you think is right and explain why you do it differently.
- Say, "Thanks, Mom. We're going to try it our way."
- Say, "We are doing what we feel is right for our situation."
- Say, "That's a good suggestion. I'll give it a try," if it's something you are willing to consider.
- Say, "Thanks, Mom, for your suggestion. We've been working on this and have tried what should work. We'll give your idea consideration."
- Acknowledge that you heard what she said. Try it if it sounds like it should work. Ignore it if not.
- Smile and thank her for her interest.
- Nicely tell her how you feel or what your doctor suggests.
- Say, "Thank you for your viewpoint. I appreciate your input. I feel comfortable doing this my own way."
- Ask for more specific information or an example of how she did it. Listen and then do what you think best.
- Say, "Oh, that's one good way, Mom. And you know what? I've learned that this is a good way, also!"

Thanks to Samara Kemp, Circle from Ceres, California

My mother-in-law cares for our five-month-old when I work. She is wonderful and my son loves her, but she is raising him in her old ways. I want her to raise him my way. What can I do?

- Discuss this problem with your spouse and share your thoughts with your mother-in-law.
- Find a job you can take your baby to.
- Talk to your spouse. Maybe you need a new sitter.
- Attend a parenting class together; define some mutual goals and set some guidelines.
- Talk to her. Tell her what you would like changed and why, and ask if she is willing to make those changes.
- Compliment her when she does what you like.
- Remember her background. Teach by doing.
- Is it possible for you to not work and to raise your son yourself?
- Find a book that you agree with, insist that she read it, and discuss it with her.
- Wait a minute! She's not raising him. You are! She's the caregiver, not the parent. Your ways will be stronger.
- Explore the possibility that the old and new ways can mix and your son will benefit from both!
- Shorten the time your son spends with Grandma, perhaps by adjusting your work schedule.

(See also I-1.)

Thanks to Sara Monser, Circle from Lafayette, California

My in-laws are coming to stay for three days. I am hesitant to ask for help, and they seem reticent to offer it. What should I do?

• Ask your spouse to ask them to share the load.
• Be really honest and say, "This is our fussy time, and I can use all the help you can give me."
• Go ahead and ask them directly. Remember that people want to help.
• Don't act "tough" and capable if they offer to help.
• Tell them that you can care for the baby, but you *really* need help with dinner.
• Ask Mom to care for the baby while you take a bath and give yourself a manicure.
• Tell Dad that you expect him to get to know his grandchild and hand him the baby.
• See to it that you get time for yourself during their visit.
• Ask. Your in-laws may be waiting for the invitation.
• Figure out something that requires two people to do—for example, one bathes the baby while the other takes the pictures.
• Take time to teach them about your house: how things work, where things go, etc.

(See also F-10.)

Thanks to Meg Murray, Circle from Lafayette, California

Grandparents buy gifts for our baby that are inappropriate. How can we get what we need for our baby?

• Tell them what your baby needs and ask them to please be helpful.
• Have a list ready with sizes, brands, and models in mind so you are ready when they talk about gifts.
• Give specific feedback, like "I really appreciated that sleeper. It's so practical."
• Say, "Sarah needs some overalls. If you happen to see some, will you pick them up for me?"
• Offer to shop with them.
• Can you exchange the gifts for things the baby needs?
• Say, "No need to bring a gift every time you wish to see your grandchild."

Thanks to Ellen Peterson, Circle from Lafayette, California

I want to use a pacifier, but the grandparents say, "Get that thing out of his mouth!" What should I do?

• He is your baby; do what you want to do.
• Listen to your doctor's recommendations on pacifiers.
• Use the pacifier when they aren't there.
• Let the grandparents see you try other comforts also.
• Read as much as you can about pacifiers. Get an article that supports your thinking and give it to the grandparents.
• You're the parent. You're in charge. The baby needs you to fulfill his needs. Do what you think best.
• Tell the grandparents that the baby's need to suck is important, and it is better to use the pacifier than to overfeed him.
• Say, "I will, when he doesn't need it anymore."

(See also D-10.)

Thanks to Judi Salts, Circle from Yakima, Washington

Grandparents are coming and I feel that I have to cook special meals and entertain them. I'm too busy.

- One night, while they are there, take them out to a special restaurant. All the rest of the time follow your regular schedule.
- Treat yourself to a cleaning service during their visit.
- Have yourself a wild, but harmless, fit over this, then sit down with your spouse and decide how to solve the problem.
- Have "tea" every afternoon with them. Otherwise, maintain your normal schedule.
- Cook doubles the week before and put half in the freezer to use when they arrive.
- Eat in the dining room and use your best china; otherwise, keep everything the same as usual.
- Grandparents are also parents; ask for help.
- Decide what you can do before they come; ask your partner for help.
- Let them treat you to dinner.
- Ask Grandmother to prepare a much-loved dinner from your childhood (or your spouse's).
- Buy frozen fancy foods.
- Send them out to sightsee or do errands for you.
- Have "rest time" for two hours a day. *Go* to your room, shut the door, and lie down. Take the baby if that works best.

(See also F-7, F-10, G-4.)

Thanks to Gail Nordeman, Circle from Healdsburg, California

H. Working Parents

How can my spouse and I balance work and family?

• Ensure family playtime.
• Communicate your needs, wants, and hopes to each other. Let go of unrealistic expectations. Decide what is most important.
• Sit down and talk about it. Find out what is right for both of you. Everyone is different.
• Both of you pitch in with the work and care of the family.
• Discuss and juggle priorities, keeping them clear. Limit outside obligations. Right now, the baby comes first.
• Hire others to do tasks that neither of you enjoys or needs to do. Use that saved time for family fun or intimacy.
• Continue talking about it. Family is work. It is the most important responsibility you have.
• Consider finding less demanding work.
• Make a special time for family and a special time for each other that fits your work schedule and your other demands.
• Guilt is a squiggle that says something is not working. Let your guilts be your guides.
• Read *The Working Parents Survival Guide* by Sally Wendkos Olds or *2001 Hints for Working Mothers* by Gloria Gilbert Mayer. (See **Resources**.)

(See also E-1, E-3, I-1.)

Thanks to Samara Kemp, Circle from Modesto, California

How can I continue breast-feeding and go back to work?

- Nurse in the morning and at night only. If you start several weeks ahead of when you go back to work, you can generally taper down your milk supply so you won't be terribly engorged your first week on the job.
- You can express your milk at work. I did it. It is time-consuming and definitely only for the highly motivated. You also need an understanding boss.
- Nurse before and after work, and express milk and freeze it for midday feedings.
- Start learning how to express milk (manually or with a breast pump) early, and try to get your baby accustomed to a bottle.
- Find a sitter near work so you can nurse at lunch.
- Schedule breaks and lunch so the baby can be brought to you.
- Investigate job-sharing, flex-time, and part-time work options.
- Get a job that allows you to take the baby with you to work. This may mean being self-employed and working at home.
- Read *Of Cradles & Careers*, by Kaye Lowman, for more ideas. (See **Resources**.)

(See also B-2, B-7, B-9.)

Thanks to Samara Kemp, Circle from Modesto, California

I am returning to work soon, and I will be leaving our baby with a wonderful caretaker. Will our baby love her more than he loves us?

- Remind yourself that babies love their mothers and fathers deeply. Love for a care provider need not decrease love for parents.
- Talk about the baby's progress with your sitter each day so that you will feel connected with what your baby is doing.
- Plan time alone with your baby each day, perhaps fifteen minutes to an hour, without other duties or distractions.
- No. The parent-child bond is stronger than we imagine.
- Babies need to make attachments. He can be bonded to you and be attached to his sitter.
- Focus on your relationship with your child and not on your child's relationship with the sitter.
- Enjoy, fully, every event you do share with your infant.
- No.
- If you are clear in your own mind that you are the parent—the most important person in that child's life—he'll know it too.

(See also D-1, D-3.)

Thanks to Ellen Peterson, Circle from Lafayette, California

Should I stay home with our baby or go back to work? How can I decide?

- Discuss this with your spouse and come to a decision together.
- Make a decision based on realities. Consider money, time, resources, your needs, and the baby's needs. Then decide.
- Trust your feelings to guide you.
- Write down the reasons to stay home, the reasons to go back to work, and weigh the options.
- Talk to parents who stayed home; talk to parents who went back to work.
- Look for ways you can do both. *Of Cradles & Careers*, by Kaye Lowman, is a good resource. (See **Resources**.)
- Stay home now; work later. This is your only chance to be home with this baby.
- Babies need happy, fulfilled parents. Look to your own well-being as well as your baby's.
- Take your time to decide.
- Stay home, at least for the first three years.
- Think of your child. Consider the quality of the child care available, and decide whether you want that person to guide your baby at this particular age.

(See also H-1, I-1, I-3.)

Thanks to Ellen Peterson, Circle from Lafayette, California

I. Who Helps with the Baby?

How do I find quality child care?

- Consider using relatives if it's possible for them to help.
- See if you can find a friend who has had the experience of caring for a baby.
- Trust your gut when you interview people.
- Ask people with kids the same age for recommendations.
- Call the state licensing agency for names of candidates, and then check the people out thoroughly.
- Call a local church and ask who the good babysitters are in the congregation.
- See if the local YMCA, YWCA, or recreation departments run babysitting courses. If they do, get lists of graduates.
- Call the local sponsor of the child-care food program. Find the sponsor through the state licensor.
- Start early. Give sitter and baby a trial run before your first day back at work.
- Visit several places several times.
- Write questions. Make a checklist.
- Drop in unexpectedly on potential caregivers.
- Join a parenting class. Ask there.
- Put an ad in your local paper. Be specific about hours, days, references.

(See also **Where to Go for Additional Support**.)

Thanks to Jean Clarke, Circle from Minneapolis, Minnesota

I feel better saying "good-bye" to my baby but she cries unless I sneak away. What should I do?

- Say "good-bye." Say it lovingly and leave.
- Give the baby a kiss instead.
- Don't be afraid of hearing your child cry when you leave.
- Call about a half-hour later if you are uncomfortable.
- Don't stay home just because she's crying. It's less traumatic if you go when you say you are going.
- If you leave with confidence, your baby will probably stop crying as soon as you go.
- Picture sitter and child happy together in your mind's eye.
- Don't sneak away. That's harder on your baby.

(See also I-3.)

Thanks to Ellen Peterson, Circle from Walnut Creek, California

What is a good age to leave an infant with a sitter?

• Have the sitter be someone you can trust—a grandmother, a good friend, another mother from a parenting class—and start before nine months.

• One week of age if all is right. Be careful of falling into the trap of saying, "It never feels right."

• Burton White says do it regularly *after* six months. (See **Resources**.)

• Any age as long as the sitter is adept and trustworthy enough to care for the child.

• When our infant was three weeks old, we left him for a few hours about once a week.

• Go with your feelings—when you feel ready.

• Look at the importance of the outing, then decide.

• Listen to your heart.

• Leave an infant with a care provider only for short periods. Save the long trips until the child is older.

Thanks to Ellen Peterson, Circle from Walnut Creek, California

I am going to a concert tonight and am leaving our infant son with a sitter. He will not take a bottle. What can I do?

• Leave an eyedropper or an infant spoon for feeding formula or breast milk.
• Try a bottle at the same temperature as human milk.
• Try formula. Not your milk.
• Feed him just before you leave and as soon as you come home.
• Have the sitter hold him as though she were breast-feeding him.
• Pump your breasts and use your own milk.
• Use an old soft nipple.
• Have sitter offer a bottle at the first sign that he is hungry.
• Call the sitter during intermission. Return home if necessary.
• Call your doctor. Ask if any infant food can be offered. If yes, get some for your sitter to give him.
• Try offering water.

(See also B-7, B-8, B-9.)

Thanks to Ellen Peterson, Circle from Sonoma, California

What do I do about my five-month-old who screams at night when I'm gone even after she's had an eight-ounce bottle of expressed milk?

• Your responsibility is to hire a sitter who knows about her screaming and can handle it. Give the sitter a few suggestions and don't worry after you are gone.

• Limit your evenings out for a couple of months and see if your daughter grows out of this.

• She may need more sucking or holding time. Try a pacifier.

• Leave more breast milk or formula if hunger is the problem. Have the caretaker give her lots of cuddling.

• Tell your caregiver to try different solutions, like a massage, or walking to classical music. Tape your voice singing a familiar lullaby, and leave the tape for your sitter to play.

• Know that this behavior doesn't last very long.

• Get a reliable, consistent caretaker whom the baby can get to know. Then go out anyway for short periods of time.

(See also A-1, A-2, A-4, A-7, I-1, I-3.)

Thanks to Samara Kemp, Circle from Turlock, California

I feel intimidated by my pediatrician and obstetrician. I don't feel like I get enough time to ask them the questions I want to ask. How can I change this?

- Say, "I would appreciate more time here." Offer to pay more if necessary.
- Write down your concerns and review your list when you talk with the doctor.
- Ask for an allotted amount of time. Know that you deserve the doctor's time.
- Think clearly about what you want. Your questions are important.
- The doctor is only another person. If you are not successful after several attempts to get all your questions answered, get a new doctor.
- Make "I" statements. "I feel...," "I need...," etc.
- Grab the doctor's hand and don't let go until you get your questions answered.
- Doctors are your employees. Remember why you've employed their services.
- Ask them to sit down, not stand, when they're talking to you.

Thanks to Nancy O'Hara, Circle from Minneapolis, Minnesota

My husband changes our baby's diapers, but that is about all. I hoped he would see things to be done and do them without being asked.

- Confront the situation. Show him a list of jobs to be done. Ask him to mark what he will do.
- Ask for help on something specific.
- Maybe he doesn't do things because he doesn't know how. Teach him.
- Give him a choice: quiet the baby or get dinner.
- If you feel mad, let him know it!
- Recognize differences in timetables and priorities, especially when he first gets home.
- Some studies show that men and women think differently and men do not "see" what needs to be done. Put the vacuum in the middle of the floor, ask him to use it, and tell him where.
- Remember, he can't read your mind.
- Talk honestly and nicely to him about the problem.
- For crying out loud, corner him and *tell* him what you need.
- Men may be caught in roles or imprisoned by images. Ask him what his dad did and what he thinks "good" dads do.
- Discuss a way for him to have a relaxing break after work—don't expect him to shift gears immediately.
- Make a list of things to be done. Discuss it. Post it. Ask him to do some of the things.

(See also E-8, F-10, F-13, J-5.)

Thanks to Ellen Peterson, Circle from Lafayette, California

J. Out and About

My infant is ten weeks old. How do I manage grocery shopping with him along?

- Put your baby in a Snugli sack, and then buckle him into his car seat. When you get to the store all you have to do is put the Snugli on because the baby is already in it.
- Bring the car seat into the store and put it in the shopping cart.
- If your baby starts fussing in the store, leave the cart in the store, take him out to the car, and feed or comfort him there. When he's settled, go back into the store and resume shopping.
- Take time to visit, getting your social needs met.
- Shop with a friend or your spouse. One holds the baby, and one shops.
- Leave the baby at home with a trusted caregiver.
- Ask your mate to do the grocery shopping.
- Make sure the baby is well fed before you go to the store.
- Dangle a toy from an infant seat in the cart.

Thanks to Ellen Peterson, Circle from Lafayette, California

We're going on a long car trip with our baby. What can we do to make it pleasant, or even tolerable?

- In many states it is a law to keep a baby in a car seat at all times for safety.
- Plan to take twice as long as usual on the road, so you can stop and take her out to feed, move about, and play.
- Take her out of the car seat at rest stops and rub her back. Rub the adults' shoulders, arms, and backs, too!
- Sit in the back seat with your baby some of the time.
- Listen to soothing music.
- Drive at night.
- If you're changing elevations, pull over and feed her when you feel ear pressure, so she will swallow and clear her ears.
- Put a sunbonnet on her to protect her from the glaring sun.
- Take some new and different toys along.
- Hang a towel on the side for protection from the sun.
- Feed the baby before you go.
- Tie toys onto the car seat, and hang pictures from the seat in front of or on hooks above the baby.
- Sing.

Thanks to Ellen Peterson, Circle from Danville, California

I'm taking my baby on an airplane. Help!

- Let the airline know you are traveling with an infant when you make reservations.
- Arrive early, early, early.
- Ask for a bulkhead seat when you make your reservations: you get more room and more privacy.
- See if an airline bassinet is available.
- Take an umbrella stroller along.
- Help your baby swallow during take off and landing by feeding him. This helps avoid pain from ear pressure.
- Fly at night.
- Ask someone to take you to the airport and help you get onto the plane.
- Ask a flight attendant to hold your meal until your hands are free to eat.
- Accept help when it is offered.
- Take new toys and a change of clothes along in the diaper bag, in addition to all the usual baby items.
- Arrange for a car seat to be available at the other end of the trip, or take yours along.

(See also J-2.)

Thanks to Ellen Peterson, Circle from Lafayette, California

Although I like to show my baby off, when I'm out for a day, I'm exhausted and I pay for it the next day with a fussy baby. What should I do?

• Try to get a good night's sleep before you go out.
• Get a sitter and leave your baby home some of the time.
• Bring a partner when you go out. It is easier to do anything when you have help.
• Shorten your list of errands. Go for an hour at a time.
• Get home by noon.
• Listen to your body during your day out. Stop *before* you are exhausted.
• Time your trip around the baby's best times.
• Plan an easy day for the day following your day out.
• Plan several small social outings over two weeks instead of a big day out.
• Watch the clock. Make visiting time shorter.
• Avoid rush hour.

(See also A-1, C-6, F-10.)

Thanks to Samara Kemp, Circle from Lafayette, California

It hardly seems worth it to go out. When my husband is taking care of the baby, he only watches her; he doesn't do anything to the house. I come home to a mess. How can I get him to share the house and baby chores?

• Go away for a day. Make a schedule of things to be done and give it to him. Ask him to see that the baby is cared for.

• If your husband won't help, get a babysitter who does help one day a week.

• Trade jobs with your husband. Tell him, "I'll mow the lawn and you take care of the baby."

• When the father cares for the baby—keep your hands off, notice what he does well, and compliment him on it.

• Ask your husband what he notices about the baby and expect him to be excited about her growth.

• Get him Klaus and Kennell's book, *Bonding: The Beginnings of Parent-Infant Attachment*, and ask him to read it because dads are so important. (See **Resources**.)

• Sunday is "my" day. I sleep in and my spouse does everything but nurse the baby, especially in the morning.

• Compliment him on everything he does well with the baby and whenever he picks up and cleans something around the house.

(See also E-8, F-10, F-13.)

Thanks to Ellen Peterson, Circle from Sonoma, California

At family gatherings our three-month-old is passed around a lot. Children especially want to hold her, but she is only content when she's in my arms. What can I do?

- Put her on the floor for everyone to enjoy.
- Set her on your lap; let others come to you to touch or play with the baby.
- To the children who want to hold the baby, say, "Yes, you may hold her. I will call you when the baby's ready."
- Tell them, "It is hard for me to quiet the baby after she gets wound up, so I'll hold her and have you touch her here."
- Say, "No thank you, she isn't ready for that yet."
- Put her in a Snugli, so it's hard to take her out.
- Strap her into an infant seat and ask that she not be taken out.
- Say, "She's too young."
- Wait until the baby is happy, and then allow her to be held only a short time.
- Only let children hold her if they aren't sick, have washed their hands, and sit cross-legged on the floor with her.

(See also K-3 and **Ages and Stages**.)

Thanks to Ellen Peterson, Circle from Lafayette, California

I am going to a conference Saturday. My husband feels unsure about feeding and caring for our infant all day, especially since I'm nursing the baby. What can I do?

- Write down what the baby usually does during the day. Give Dad the schedule as a guideline.
- Remember that the baby won't starve himself.
- Babies often take bottles better when Mother is not around.
- Let your husband know that you trust him to care for the baby and that he doesn't have to do everything exactly the way you do it.
- Let them have a couple of hours of practice ahead of time with you out of the house.
- Call home and encourage him.
- Express milk ahead of time so that your husband can give it to your baby.
- Let him know that the baby cries when you are taking care of him, too.
- Don't call home. Trust him to cope and to get to know his baby.
- Let your husband practice bottle-feeding the baby using breast milk and perhaps trying several different nipples.
- Ask him if he has any questions for you before you go.

(See also A-1, B-7, D-8, F-12, I-7.)

Thanks to Ellen Peterson, Circle from Lafayette, California

K. Second-Baby Blues

We are expecting our second baby, and I'm worried that I don't have enough love for two. What can I do?

- Light a candle. Light another from it. Light one for each of you. See that the light is not diminished by each addition. Rather, it is increased.
- After baby comes, set aside a time for your two-year-old and your spouse.
- I have two children and had the same fear. Now I bask in the love my two sons have for each other.
- Remember that there is always enough love. Do not confuse time with love.
- Remember to show your love through touching.
- Children don't need to compete for our love and attention. We can teach them to compete or not to compete.
- Set aside time to love yourself so that your needs are met.
- Eliminate outside pressures so your love has room to flow.
- Be confident that love begets more love.
- Affirm yourself that you are capable and can love many people at the same time.
- Rely on your personal experiences: Count the people you've added to your heart and know there's always room for more.

(See also F-10.)

Thanks to Samara Kemp, Circle from Lafayette, California

After our first child was born, my husband was helping a lot. He doesn't seem as interested in this new baby and stays at work late. What can I do?

- Tell him you need his help even more than you did with your first baby. Make sure he hears you.
- Ask him if he will spend twenty minutes with each of the children three or four times a week so both you and he can have twenty minutes alone with each child frequently.
- Let him know that you appreciate his wanting to be a good provider. Remind him that his children need love and attention as well as money.
- Ask him to help with the older child.
- Confront him. Ask for very specific contracts: "I will be home on Tuesday by 6:00 P.M. to care for both children for two hours."
- Don't let him get by with this stuff.
- Sounds like a serious problem between the two of you. Talk it out and decide together how you can both get more of what you need.
- Perhaps he is at such a place in his career and company that he has little left over to give to his family. This is a dilemma that he can solve with encouragement from you.

(See also D-1, E-6, E-8, F-10, F-12, I-7, J-5.)

Thanks to Jean Clarke, Circle from Wayzata, Minnesota

How can I protect my infant from our older children?

• Teach the older children where it is OK to touch and where it's not OK.

• Set clear limits for the older children and follow through.

• Give the older children another way to show their feelings (especially their negative ones) for the infant. (Hit the pillow, *not* the baby; touch gently, etc.)

• Help the older children feel loved by spending fifteen minutes a day alone with each.

• Put the baby in a safe place and keep an eye on the other kids.

• Teach the older children how to be with the baby. For instance, say "Hold out your finger and the baby will grab hold," or, "Touch or pat the baby very gently." Let them practice with you.

• Tell them about how you (or someone) protected them as babies and how you taught others to touch them in the right way.

• Read or tell them stories about when they were little and vulnerable. Show them their own baby pictures.

• Keep the infant with you in a Snugli pack.

• Get Karen Hendrickson's *Baby and I Can Play*. Read it with the older children and talk about it. (See **Resources**.)

(See also J-6.)

Thanks to Jean Clarke, Circle from Minneapolis, Minnesota

What can I do so I'm not "torn apart" by two children who both want Mommy?

- Involve the older child in helping with the little one.
- Read to the older one while you nurse the baby.
- Get your spouse or another adult to take one child for a while so you can spend time with the other one; then switch, so you get individual time with each.
- Make sure you are not encouraging the children to compete for your attention by comparing them.
- Think about whether you are subtly encouraging the children in this behavior because you want to feel wanted. If so, find another way to feel worthwhile.
- Coping with this is part of learning to live with two kids rather than one. Know that you can't be perfect but can learn to do a good job.
- Say to yourself, "I have enough love, strength, etc., to give. I am enough."

(See also K-1, K-3.)

Thanks to Jean Clarke, Circle from Plymouth, Minnesota

Where to Go for Additional Support

If you have talked with your family and friends, tried the ideas in the Suggestion Circles, read some child-rearing books, and still feel stuck with a problem, here are some places to call for additional help or to find out about parenting classes. If you have difficulty finding a telephone number after looking in both the white and the yellow pages, call any of these sources and ask them to help you find the number you need.

Community Services

Parent-education organizations
La Leche League or other breast-feeding support groups
Childbirth education groups
YMCA, YWCA, or a local church or synagogue
Chemical abuse treatment centers
Chemical abuse prevention programs
Women's or men's support groups
Battered women's and children's shelters
Parental stress hot-lines
Alcoholics Anonymous
Parents Anonymous

Schools

Community education (local school district)
Colleges or universities
Community or junior colleges
Vocational and technical schools

Government

Community mental health organizations
Public health nurse or department
Child protection service
Family service agencies
County social service agencies

Private Services

Psychologists, social workers, psychiatrists, therapists, family counselors

Interview the persons who will help you to see if they know about the area in which you need help. If you don't get what you need, go somewhere else until you do.

—The Editors

How to Lead a Suggestion Circle

To lead a Suggestion Circle in a group to which you belong, do the following:

1. Ask the parent who is volunteering a problem to state it in specific terms.
2. Remind the group of the rules: don't discuss the problem; each person offers one short quality suggestion; pass if you want to; go around the Circle in order; don't judge or evaluate the suggestions; ask the person who requested the Circle to say "thank you!" after each suggestion and then take the ideas and decide, at a later time, what will be helpful.
3. Ask a member of the group to write down the suggestions and give them to the person who requested the Circle.

A Circle of ten people takes three or four minutes to complete. Circles may also be run by following the same rules and calling eight to twelve friends on the phone. State the problem concisely. Ask for one quality suggestion from each friend. Thank your phone participant for the suggestion or pass. Say "good-bye" and call the next person.

—Gail Nordeman

Conclusion

Parents look back on their first six months with a baby with a sigh. They think of the exhaustion and hard work involved, yet they cherish the special excitement of getting to know a new soul and starting to build a new family system that includes this baby.

This book, and the ideas in it, originated from the editors' belief that new parents deserve help and support with this important job of becoming capable and loving parents who make good decisions for their babies and themselves.

Infants who are given responsive care during the first six months develop a strong base from which to move out and enjoy the world. They can be confident and curious as they wiggle out of our arms and into everything. When a dad and a mom have accepted their baby for all that she is, have enjoyed holding her, and have not rushed her to grow up fast, she will move out in her own time.

New challenges face parents with each developmental stage. This is the first in a series of *HELP!* books that you can use as your family grows. Remember that you don't have to be perfect to be a good parent, only willing to learn and to love.

—Ellen Peterson

Resources

Badger, Earladeen. *Infant Toddler: Introducing Your Child to the Joy of Learning.* Englewood Cliffs, N.J.: McGraw-Hill, 1981.

Berends, Polly Berrien. *Whole Child/Whole Parent.* New York: Harper & Row, 1983.

Bolles, Richard. *The Three Boxes of Life and How to Get Out of Them.* Berkeley: Ten Speed Press, 1978.

Brazelton, T. Berry, M.D. *Infants and Mothers.* New York: Dell, 1983.

Briggs, Dorothy. *Your Child's Self-Esteem.* Garden City, N.Y.: Doubleday, 1970.

Buscaglia, Leo. *Living, Loving and Learning.* Greenwich, Conn.: Fawcett, 1983.

Caplan, Frank. *First Twelve Months of Life.* New York: Bantam Books, 1973.

Carson, Mary B. *The Womanly Art of Breastfeeding.* Franklin Park, Ill.: La Leche League International, 1983.

Clarke, Jean Illsley. *Self-Esteem: A Family Affair.* Minneapolis: Winston Press, 1978.

_____. *Ouch, That Hurts! A Handbook for People Who Hate Criticism.* Plymouth, Minn.: Daisy Press, 1983.

_____. *The Important Infants.* Plymouth, Minn.: Daisy Tapes, 1983. (16535 9th Ave. N. 55447)

Dodson, Dr. Fitzhugh. *How to Father.* New York: NAL, 1975.

Eiger, Marvin, and Olds, Sally. *Complete Book of Breastfeeding*. New York: Bantam Books, 1973.

Fonda, Jane. *Workout for Pregnancy, Birth, and Recovery*. New York: Simon & Schuster, 1982.

Fraiberg, Selma H. *The Magic Years*. New York: Scribner, 1959.

Galinsky, Ellen. *Between Generations: The Six Stages of Parenthood*. New York: New York Times Books, 1981.

Greene, Bob. *Good Morning, Merry Sunshine*. New York: Atheneum, 1984.

Greenleaf, Barbara Kaye. *Help: A Handbook for Working Mothers*. New York: Berkley Books, 1979.

Hagstrom, Julie, and Morrill, Joan. *Games Babies Play*. New York: A & W Visual Library, 1979.

Hendricks, Gay. *The Centering Book*. Englewood Cliffs, N.J.: Prentice-Hall, 1977.

Hendrickson, Karen. *Baby and I Can Play*. Seattle: Parenting Press, 1985.

Jones, Sandy. *Crying Baby, Sleepless Nights*. New York: Warner Books, 1983.

Karnes, Merle B. *You and Your Small Wonder*. Circle Pines, Minn.: American Guidance Service, 1982.

Klaus, Marshall H., and Kennell, John H. *Bonding: The Beginnings of Parent-Infant Attachment*. Mosby, N.Y.: Johnson & Johnson, 1982.

Lakein, Alan. *How to Get Control of Your Time & Your Life*. New York: NAL, 1974.

126

Leach, Penelope. *Your Baby & Child from Birth to Age Five*. New York: Alfred A. Knopf, 1974.

_____. *Babyhood*. New York: Alfred A. Knopf, 1983.

Levin, Pamela. *Becoming the Way We Are*. Wenatchee, Wash.: Directed Media, 1974.

Lowman, Kaye. *Of Cradles & Careers: A Guide to Reshaping Your Job to Include a Baby in Your Life*. Franklin Park, Ill.: La Leche League International, 1984.

Lowndes, Marion. *A Manual for Babysitters*. Boston: Little Brown, 1974.

Mayer, Gloria Gilbert. *2001 Hints for Working Mothers*. New York: Quill, 1983.

Olds, Sally Wendkos. *The Working Parents' Survival Guide*. New York: Bantam Books, 1983.

Pryor, Karen. *Nursing Your Baby*. New York: Pocket Books, 1984.

Rozdilsky, Mary Lou, and Banet, Barbara. *What Now? A Handbook for New Parents*. New York: Scribner, 1972.

Spock, Benjamin. *Baby and Child Care*. New York: Pocket Books, 1985.

White, Burton L. *The First Three Years of Life*. New York: Avon Books, 1975.

Magazines, Newsletters

Dads Only, P.O. Box 340, Julian, CA 92036. Monthly newsletter filled with suggestions to help dads interact with kids and wives.

Growing Child, 22 N. Second St., Lafayette, IN 47902. Monthly guide to growth and development coordinated to your baby's birthdate.

Mothering, P.O. Box 2208, Albuquerque, NM 87103. Quarterly. Mothering as an art with guidance toward a simpler lifestyle.

Parents Magazine, 685 Third Ave., New York, NY 10017. Monthly. Covers topics through school years to adolescence.

Practical Parenting, 18326A Minnetonka Blvd., Deephaven, MN 55391. Bimonthly newsletter. Lots of tips collected from parents.

Working Mother, 230 Park Ave., New York, NY 10169. Monthly. Covers issues about careers and families.

About the Editors

Jean Illsley Clarke is the author of *Self- Esteem: A Family Affair* and the creator of the parenting program of the same name. The Suggestion Circle technique comes from that program. Jean is a Transactional Analyst, a parent educator, and a mother of three. She holds a Master of Arts in Human Development and an honorary doctorate of Human Services. She likes being with infants and the parents of infants.

Samara I. Kemp, R.N., B.S.N., has been a single parent since 1974. Her four children range in ages from twelve to twenty-two. Professionally, she cares for newborn infants, teaches holistic health techniques for optimum health, and leads parenting and childbirth education courses. Her beliefs are that infants are people in small bodies, that parents have rights as individuals, and that each of us has all the answers, which are obtained through centered quietness.

Gail A. Nordeman, B.A., is a mother of five children; a cofounder and director of A Growing Place, an Educational and Counseling Center, in Cincinnati, Ohio; and is a registered nurse with a Clinical Provisional Teaching Membership in the International Transactional Analysis Association. She taught childbirth as well as mother and baby-care classes for the American Red Cross for over fifteen years.

Ellen Reese Peterson, B.A., Lifetime Credential Teacher, State of California, has over eighteen years' experience in education and is cofounder of The Nurture Company, a nonprofit parent education organization in Lafayette, California. She is the mother of two children, and she has been facilitating groups of parents and their newborn infants since 1978. She also leads "Self-Esteem: A Family Affair" classes, as well as workshops on discipline and sharing joy. From her own experience, she values parental growth and development as much as she believes in children's growth and development.

Index

Other Learning Materials Available

Developmental Tapes, by Jean Illsley Clarke. These audio cassette tapes present important information about children and the nurturing they need. Told in entertaining and easy-to-understand language from the perspective of children of different ages, the tapes describe child care by parents and by day-care providers. The stories allow adults to set aside fear or guilt and have the distance they may need to hear the information presented. The tapes, told in both male and female voices, are also useful tools for helping older children understand their little brother's and sister's needs and behavior. Each story is twelve-to-eighteen minutes long; at least eight spaced listenings are recommended.

Ups and Downs with Feelings, by Carole Gesme. This collection of games features a game board with a wide variety of "feeling faces" to help children and adults identify feelings and learn ways to be responsible for them. Included are directions for seven separate games, one of which uses the affirmations printed in this book.

Affirmation Cards. Tiny colored cards, with a separate affirmation printed on each, that can be read, carried, or given as gifts.

For more information, including prices, write to

Daisy Press
16535 Ninth Avenue North
Plymouth, MN 55447